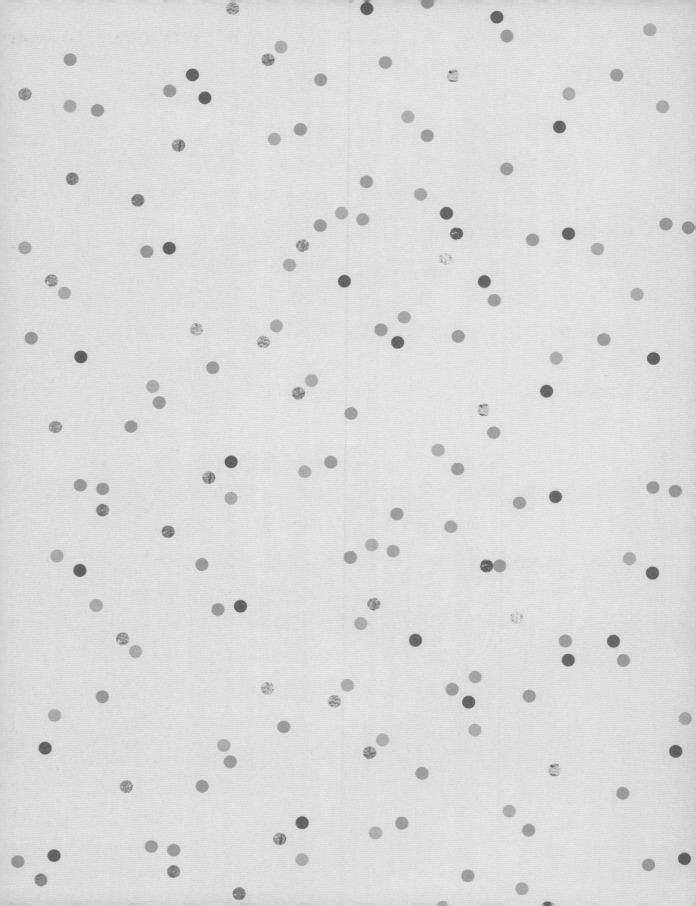

BAKE
MY
DAY

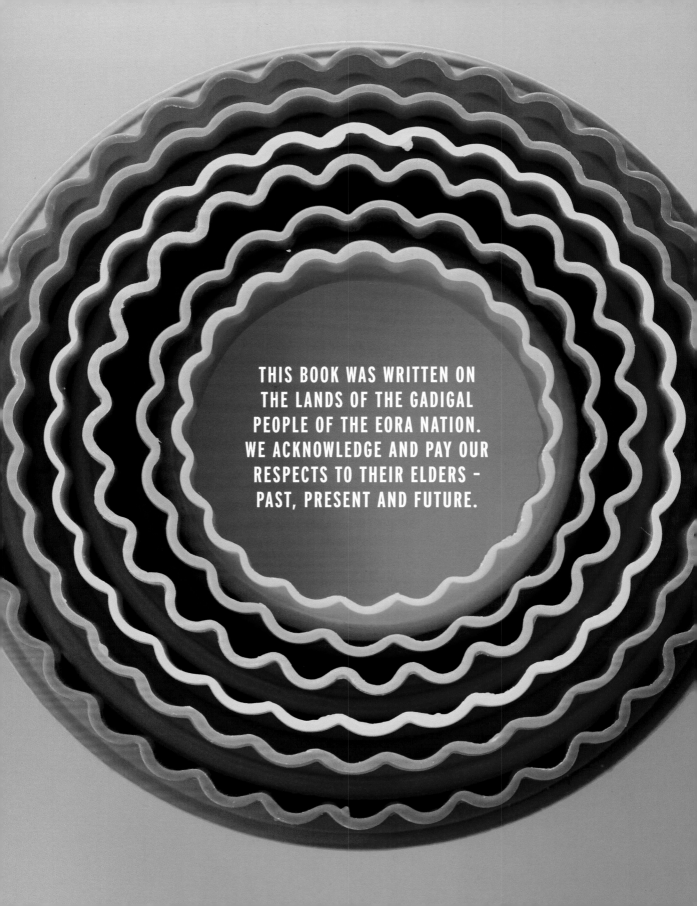

BAKE MY DAY

KATHERINE SABBATH

murdoch books

Sydney | London

contents

CHAPTER 1

sweetly simple
16

CHAPTER 2

flex your spatula
50

CHAPTER 3

next level 120

CHAPTER 4

essential elements 216

hello friends

I've always enthusiastically believed home bakers are the best kinds of friends. You see, we home bakers come as a sweet package – a special part of our personality is devoted to conjuring up sweet ways to make friends.

Bake My Day is here to arm you with an arsenal of scrumptious creations that will inject delight into any get-together. In these pages you will find all my beloved bakes and recipes from the times I've successfully impressed friends — whipped up with all my favourite flavours and ingredients (including large amounts of chocolate and buttercream!). I've also included a few recipes that my loved ones have whipped up to woo me, because sharing in cheeky treats is crucial to any long-lasting friendship.

There's something very simple yet valuable in the ceremony of considerate gift-giving, and baking is a skill that encompasses this and so much more. The process of creating, learning and experimenting with new ideas is extremely satisfying. As an introvert who lacks confidence when meeting new people, I've also found that baking can be a powerful way to connect with others; turning up to a party with a knockout cake or a plate of brownies always makes a good impression! I'm yet to meet anyone who's left in a bad mood after someone's gone to the effort of making them a specially baked treat. A friendly home baker (aka cake dealer) always has the ability to make the world a better place.

Since my last cookbook in 2019, a fantastically kitschy and enthusiastic ode to Australiana called *Bake Australia Great*, I've rather fortuitously become the new owner of Creative Cake Decorating, a premium Australian-made food colouring and cake decorating products company. I now work there most days making our products by hand, and I love helping dessert-lovers worldwide bring their creations to life.

Bake My Day has been created to suit any skill level, because dessert should be enjoyed by everyone. Start off with any of the many deliciously simple recipes and slowly work your way up to the showstoppers. You'll be a baking genius in no time.

I'm incredibly chuffed knowing this book will help you celebrate all that is great about creative baking and sharing in this fun with others. It has been conceptualised, written and taste-tested (repeatedly by friends and family) right here in my home. Hopefully it will become your best mate in the kitchen, with easy-to-follow recipes plus loads of tips and tricks to make your next masterpiece come to life.

Feel free to mix and match recipe components to tailor each creation. Once you learn the basics of baking and have a handful of trusty recipes that you can adapt to cater for any occasion or tastebuds, the dessert world is your oyster.

Some of my most interesting cakes were inspired by my favourite things, such as nostalgic flavours from my childhood (with Vietnamese and German influences featuring heavily), as well as art, fashion, nature and architecture. Inspiration can come from anywhere, including the confectionery aisle of the local supermarket, where I always find exciting bits and bobs. Feel free to use whatever you have in the cupboard, whether it's left-over sprinkles, chunks of honeycomb, chopped-up jersey caramels or colourful meringues (which look awesome when crushed).

Keep this book of bakes under your wing for the next staff morning tea, local fundraiser or birthday party, and your friends, family, colleagues and sweet-toothed community will rejoice. The following recipes will help you spread happiness, make friends and be the life of the party. So preheat your oven, grease your tins, throw on your apron and test out your cakeabilities!

bake like a boss

Pour yourself a cuppa and take a breather while you read these nifty tips for baking with minimum fuss. These simple tricks will help you avoid common missteps, which have the tendency to compound into even bigger and not-so-pleasant baking experiences. So wield that whisk and spatula fearlessly and, most importantly, have a blast!

1 BE PREPARED

Avoid a last-minute dash to the supermarket by making sure you have everything you need before you start baking. It's always a good idea to read over the whole recipe before you start, so you know how many steps it involves and how long it might take. A timeline can be a really useful tool if multiple steps (e.g. baking, frosting and decorating) are involved. This will ensure you've given yourself enough time to complete each step.

2 USE CAKE FLOUR

Cake flour gives a much more delicate and fluffy texture to cakes and biscuits. This is because cake flour is lower in protein than regular flour, so you're less likely to over-mix the batter and develop too much gluten. You can make your own cake flour (see p. 227), but it's readily available in most supermarkets and specialty grocers. And if you really can't get your hands on it, it's not the end of the world; regular flour will work fine, it will just result in a denser cake.

3 BE MINDFUL OF TEMPERATURE

You'll notice that I use most refrigerated ingredients at room temperature. I've found that when all the ingredients are close to the same temperature, they mix together easily and evenly, and produce a more uniform texture.

4 CHEAT IF YOU HAVE TO

Want to bake a show-stopping layer cake but don't want the fuss? If you prefer not to have to worry about levelling your cakes, simply divide the batter evenly into individual cake tins to make the layers (which will require a shorter bake time) rather than baking one big cake. Alternatively, invest in a cake levelling tool, which will do the work of neatly slicing your cake layers. You can also use a long, thin knife to cut the layers.

Don't be ashamed to use packet cake mixes if you're pressed for time or if you find you're really struggling with the whole cake baking experience. Packet cake mixes were my mainstay when I started baking in primary school (and well into my adolescence). I even use them now sometimes when the gourmet ones are on special! To me, some of the cheaper brands taste overly sweet and 'fake', but they certainly played a role in igniting my passion for baking!

5 CHECK YOUR CAKE

All oven temperatures used in this book are for a fan-forced oven; I find that this gives the best results. (If using a conventional oven, you will need to increase the temperature given by 20°C.) Be aware that not all ovens are created equal and this can sometimes result in lopsided, domed or uneven cakes. Placing your cake in the centre of the oven will allow for even airflow and ultimately more even cooking. For a more level cake, it's worth rotating your cake halfway around, two-thirds of the way through the cooking time. You can buy 'bake even' strips to ensure even baking results, or make your own by soaking strips of cotton (like an old kitchen towel) in cold water and wrapping these in foil to form an insulated collar around the outside of the cake tin.

6 PRACTISE

Practice makes perfect! As with any skill, when it comes to cake baking and decorating, the more you practise (and the more mistakes you make), the more opportunities you will have to learn. Every baker has had their fair share of kitchen disasters (I am certainly guilty of some horrors in the kitchen), but once you've picked yourself up and wiped up the mess, you're not likely to make the same mistake again.

planning ahead

When it comes to making cakes – especially elaborately decorated ones – I like to follow the motto: Be Prepared. If you're making a cake for a big occasion, it's a good idea to bake the cake and/or prepare the frosting a few days in advance. This leaves you more time to decorate the cake on the big day, and it also allows time for you to start again in the event of a baking disaster (I have certainly had my share of those!).

When serving your cakes, it's important to note that cakes containing cream cheese frosting or buttercream are best brought to room temperature first – there's nothing pleasant about hoeing into a mouthful of solid, cold buttercream!

CAKES

As a general rule of thumb, most cakes can be baked a few days in advance. Once the cake is completely cool, tightly wrap it in two layers of plastic wrap before storing as indicated below.

Sponge cake: Bake up to 2 days in advance and store at room temperature or in the refrigerator.

Mudcake: Bake up to 4 days in advance and store at room temperature or in the refrigerator.

Choc-heaven cake: Bake up to 3 days in advance and store in the refrigerator.

Dark chocolate sea salt cake: Bake up to 2 days in advance and store at room temperature.

Violet velvet cake/red velvet cake: Bake up to 1 day in advance and store at room temperature.

Meringue: Bake up to 1 week in advance and store in an airtight container at room temperature.

FREEZING CAKES

The cakes listed above (except meringue) can be frozen for up to 2 months (mudcakes can be frozen for up to 3 months). Once the cake is completely cool, tightly wrap the whole cake (or wrap each individual layer, if it's a layer cake) in two layers of plastic wrap and then place it in an airtight container or freezer bag. Thaw the cake overnight in the refrigerator before decorating.

FROSTINGS, TOPPINGS & FILLINGS

Preparing frostings, toppings and fillings in advance is a real time-saver, and you can store them in an airtight container in the refrigerator or freezer. Thaw frozen buttercream or cream cheese frosting overnight in the refrigerator, then bring to room temperature (gently reheat in the microwave in 20-second bursts if needed). Beat the buttercream or cream cheese frosting on low speed until smooth before applying to your cake.

Buttercream: Refrigerate for up to 10 days or freeze for up to 2 months.

Swiss meringue buttercream: Refrigerate for up to 10 days or freeze for up to 2 months.

Cream cheese frosting: Refrigerate for up to 5 days or freeze for up to 1 month.

Ganache: Refrigerate for up to 7 days or freeze for up to 1 month. (Cover the surface with plastic wrap before storing.)

Salted caramel: Refrigerate for up to 2 weeks or freeze for up to 2 months.

Lemon curd: Refrigerate for up to 1 week.

COOKIES

Most cookies can be stored in an airtight container in a cool, dry place for up to 5 days, in the fridge for up to 2 weeks or frozen for up to 2 months. In some cases (see individual recipes), cookie dough can be frozen — just freeze the balls in a resealable plastic bag and bake from frozen for an extra 5 minutes.

cakes on
the move

Transporting your amazing creation is possibly the most anxiety-inducing stage of every baker's journey. While you can't control everything, here are the tips I swear by to help keep a cake intact during its maiden voyage out into the big bad world!

1 Firstly, avoid soft fillings if you know in advance you'll need to transport the cake. Buttercream works fantastically as the stiff layers hold your cake together. However, a soft, loose filling such as whipped cream may not be the best idea. If a component of the filling is soft, like a fruit compote, caramel, curd or jam, be sure to put a border of buttercream around the edge of each layer, before loading the centre with the soft filling. This will hold the cake layers up and also keep the filling from sliding around too much; think of it as a fence or dam to hold in your filling. This will make your cake much sturdier and easier to transport (see p. 221 for step-by-step instructions on this method). If the weather is hot, keep the cake in the refrigerator right up until you need to leave, then blast the air conditioner in the car and be sure to dress warmly — you want the car to feel like the inside of a refrigerator! If your journey is longer than 4 hours, consider using a filling that doesn't require refrigeration.

2 Think about how your decorations will hold up while you're on the move. I generally choose a decorating method that is conducive to travel, such as stiff buttercream ruffles or smaller decorations like wafer flowers or sprinkles which can be easily held in place. If you're using fragile or larger decorations such as fresh flowers, meringues or chocolate, it's best to add these after you have arrived at your destination. Not only will it make travelling less stressful, but it will ensure that your cake looks perfect when served.

3 If you are planning to transport a tiered cake, you will need to construct the cake well to ensure it arrives at the destination safely. Using internal cake supports is essential to building any stacked cake. Cake supports are placed inside a cake: pressed into the bottom layer after it has been assembled. If you were to skip the cake supports, the top cake may slowly sink into the bottom as the weight is too much to hold. Cake supports hold all the weight, making the cake easier to transport (see p. 224 for my tips on how to stack a tiered buttercream cake).

4 If you are transporting a smaller cake over long distances, get a sturdy box to put the cake in (or invest in a professional cake carrier). The board or plate that the cake is on should be touching the sides of the box so that it does not slide around inside as you travel. Rather than lower the cake inside the box, I use a box cutter to open up one side of the box so that the cake can easily slide in and out. Use packing tape to close the side of the box back up again before travelling.

5 When you place a cake in the back of a car (I usually place my cakes in the clean boot of my car), whether in a box or just stacked on a cake board, you want to make sure it doesn't move around as you drive. The easiest way to do this is to place the cake or box on top of a non-slip mat. The best option is a silicone baking mat that is larger than your cake. Put the mat down first and then place the cake on top of it. The non-slip mat will prevent the cake from sliding around as you drive and ensure that your cake arrives safely! If you do not have a silicone baking mat, use a silicone pot holder, a yoga mat or even a rubber cabinet liner. Anything that will help grip the cake (rubber, silicone, plastic, etc) will work. And of course, no sudden braking!

baker's kitchen kit

A well-equipped kitchen makes baking a breeze. In addition to basic kitchen utensils, mixing bowls and appliances, the following tools and equipment will make the wonderful process of creating and baking easier and more enjoyable:

- a candy thermometer
- a cake leveller or a long, thin knife for slicing cakes into layers
- a stable and smooth-spinning cake turntable or lazy Susan (this will save both your time and your sanity when it comes to frosting a cake!)
- cake scrapers of varying heights
- offset metal spatulas in varying sizes
- basic piping tips and piping bags (you can find reusable and/or biodegradable piping bags in cake decorating supply stores)
- gel paste food colouring (for colouring cakes, meringue, buttercream, fondant and ganache)
- oil-based or powdered food colouring (for colouring chocolate).

A pantry with a happy assortment of sprinkles and candies is a pure delight. I like to combine different types to make fun mixtures. Look in confectionery stores, cake decorating stores and online for different and unusual sprinkles and lollies.

Of course, when baking, the most important tool of all is the oven. As every oven is slightly different, an oven thermometer may be a good investment. This will allow you to check that your oven is calibrated to the correct temperature, investigate any 'hot spots' in the oven, or check to see if it loses heat quickly when the door is opened. The thermometer will guide you in adjusting the temperature or baking times accordingly. Check the manufacturer's instructions for best results, and get to know and understand your oven's nuances through lots of good baking practise!

It's important to use accurate scales, measuring spoons, cups and jugs. I use Australian standard metric measurements, but have also included imperial conversions in the recipes. Note that 1 Australian tablespoon is equal to 20 ml, whereas 1 imperial tablespoon is equal to 15 ml. If you are using an imperial tablespoon, adjust your measurements accordingly.

CHAPTER 1

.....

sweetly simple

.....

**Simple sweet treats to build confidence...
a great place to start for beginner bakers**

MAMA YEN'S CARAMEL DREAMS

SERVES 6

Of all the desserts I ate growing up around my extended Vietnamese family, *banh flan* (aka Vietnamese crème caramel) was always a well-loved favourite. As a kid I was just so delighted by the wobbly, jelly-like texture – and aromatic caramel syrup is like honey to a bear for a child! This decadent, lightly sweet dessert is made with eggs, sugar and just a hint of coffee, creating a rich texture.

CARAMEL

¾ cup (165 g) caster (superfine) sugar

squeeze of lime juice

1 Grease six ¾ cup (185 ml) heatproof ramekins or dariole moulds and place them in a roasting pan.

2 Combine the caster sugar and 2 tablespoons water in a small saucepan and use a wooden spoon to stir over low heat until the sugar dissolves. Increase the heat to medium and bring to the boil. Boil for about 10 minutes without stirring, brushing down the side of the saucepan with a pastry brush dipped in water to dissolve any sugar crystals, until the mixture turns a deep caramel colour. Remove immediately from the heat and carefully add ¼ cup (60 ml) water, plus the lime juice.

3 Return to the heat and bring to a simmer, swirling the pan occasionally and stirring with a wooden spoon if necessary, until the caramel is smooth. Pour the caramel into the ramekins, dividing evenly. Set aside at room temperature for 30 minutes, or until the caramel is set.

CUSTARD

1 vanilla bean, split lengthways

1 cup (250 ml) milk

5 large eggs, at room temperature

⅓ cup (75 g) firmly packed soft brown sugar

3 teaspoons instant coffee (optional)

400 ml (14 fl oz) tinned coconut milk

1 Preheat the oven to 160°C (315°F) fan-forced. Scrape the vanilla seeds from the bean and combine the pod, seeds and milk in a small saucepan. Bring to a simmer over medium heat. Remove from the heat as soon as it starts to simmer and set aside to cool.

2 In a large bowl, use a balloon whisk to whisk together the eggs, brown sugar and instant coffee until well combined. Remove the vanilla pod from the milk and then whisk the milk into the egg mixture along with the coconut milk. Pour the mixture through a fine sieve into a jug.

3 Gently pour the custard mixture into the ramekins over the caramel. Add enough boiling water to the roasting pan to reach halfway up the sides of the ramekins. Bake for 35 minutes, or until the custards are set but still wobble slightly when shaken.

4 Remove the ramekins from the roasting pan and set aside for 1 hour, or until cooled to room temperature. Cover the ramekins with plastic wrap and refrigerate for 2 hours, or until well chilled.

5 To serve, use your fingertips to gently pull the top of the custard away from the outside of the ramekin towards the centre. Invert onto a serving plate and shake gently to release. Serve immediately.

STORAGE

These *banh flan* will keep unmoulded and covered with plastic wrap in the refrigerator for up to 2 days.

CRACK FOR CHOCOLATE LOVERS

MAKES 18

Reminiscent of that perfect chocolate brownie, these cookies are irresistible with their crisp, crackled exteriors and chewy, fudgy centres. The toasted buttery macadamia nuts are an extra level of yum! The perfect texture of these cookies relies on resting the batter as directed.

....

1½ cups (185 g) icing (confectioners') sugar

½ cup (55 g) unsweetened cocoa (I used dark cocoa made from alkalised cacao beans, which you can buy from cake decorating stores, but Dutch or natural/untreated is also fine)

⅛ teaspoon sea salt

¼ cup (2–2½) egg whites, at room temperature, plus 2 tablespoons extra (pasteurised egg whites are available in cartons at most major supermarkets)

2 tablespoons vegetable oil or melted coconut oil

2 teaspoons vanilla extract

1 cup (120 g) macadamia nut pieces, plus extra to decorate

2 pinches sea salt flakes, for sprinkling (optional)

1   Preheat the oven to 170°C (325°F) fan-forced. Line two large baking trays with baking paper and lightly spray with cooking oil spray (these cookies are extremely sticky and benefit from the extra greasing).

2   Using a hand-held mixer or a stand mixer, whisk together the icing sugar, cocoa and salt. Add ¼ cup (60 ml) of egg whites (two whites), the oil and the vanilla extract and mix on low speed. Increase the speed to medium as the sugar and cocoa are absorbed into the liquid. The mixture should be very thick. If the mixture looks too dry, beat in additional egg white 1 tablespoon at a time. Add the macadamia pieces and fold together using a silicone spatula. Allow the batter to rest for 15 minutes. The cookie batter should be thick and viscous.

3   Use a tablespoon to scoop the mixture onto the baking trays 2½ cm (1 inch) apart. Embed the top of each cookie with the additional macadamia pieces. Allow the unbaked cookies to rest on the baking trays for 5 minutes more.

4   Bake for 10–12 minutes, or until the tops are glossy and crackled. Watch them carefully so they don't over-bake, especially if your oven tends to run hot. Allow the cookies to cool on the baking trays. While cooling, sprinkle with sea salt flakes (if using). When the cookies are completely cooled, gently peel them from the baking paper. They will be soft and delicate, so do this carefully.

CARAMEL-FIX BLONDIES

MAKES 20

Rich, buttery and chunky bars of deliciousness! Blondies can be flavoured in all sorts of ways and lend themselves to being the perfect gifts and travelling snacks. In this recipe I've added some salty elements to dance alongside the sweet, and packed in some crunch and exciting bits!

2 cups (300 g) plain (all-purpose) flour

½ teaspoon baking powder

½ teaspoon sea salt

165 g (5¾ oz) unsalted butter, at room temperature

1¾ cups (385 g) firmly packed soft brown sugar

2 large eggs, at room temperature

2 teaspoons vanilla bean paste

⅔ cup (100 g) caramel chocolate chips (if you can't find these, use white chocolate chips or peanut butter chips)

¾ cup (125 g) dark chocolate chips

⅔ cup (50 g) pretzels, broken into coarse pieces

pinch sea salt flakes, for sprinkling (optional)

1 Preheat the oven to 170°C (325°F) fan-forced. Grease a 23 cm (9 inch) square baking tin, at least 5 cm (2 inches) deep, and line with baking paper.

2 In a medium bowl, whisk together the flour, baking powder and salt.

3 Using a hand-held mixer or a stand mixer fitted with the paddle attachment, beat the butter and sugar on medium speed for 3 minutes, or until light and fluffy. Add the eggs and vanilla, mixing until well combined.

4 Gradually add the dry ingredients and mix until just combined. Stir in the caramel chocolate chips, dark chocolate chips and pretzel pieces.

5 Spread the batter into the prepared tin. Bake for 35 minutes, or until a toothpick inserted in the centre comes out clean. If desired, top immediately with a little sprinkling of sea salt flakes.

6 Stand the tin on a baking rack to allow it to cool completely before turning out and cutting into bars.

STORAGE

These blondies can be stored in an airtight container in a cool, dry place for up to 4 days, in the refrigerator for up to 1 week, or in the freezer for up to 3 months.

WHOA MAMA! CHOC CHIP COOKIES

MAKES 40

My favourite treat of all time is a chewy choc-chip cookie. I'm yet to meet anyone who doesn't love cookies (do these people exist?). The dough for these cookies is refrigerated for 24–36 hours before baking, which makes for a more complex, toffee-like flavour and a greater variation in texture when it comes to crispiness, chewiness and fudginess. Sea salt, which accentuates the rich chocolate flavour, is the finishing touch.

1⅔ cups (250 g) plain (all-purpose) cake flour or plain (all-purpose) flour

1⅔ cups (250 g) bread flour

1½ teaspoons bicarbonate of soda (baking soda)

1½ teaspoons baking powder

1 teaspoon sea salt

280 g (10 oz) unsalted butter, at room temperature

1¼ cups (280 g) firmly packed soft brown sugar

1 cup (220 g) caster (superfine) sugar

2 large eggs, at room temperature

2 teaspoons vanilla bean paste

550 g (1 lb 4 oz) good quality dark chocolate (at least 60% cocoa), chopped

3 generous pinches of sea salt flakes, for sprinkling

1 Sift the flours, bicarbonate of soda, baking powder and salt into a bowl. Set aside.

2 Using a hand-held mixer or a stand mixer fitted with the paddle attachment, beat the butter and sugars on medium speed for 3 minutes, or until light and fluffy.

3 Add the eggs one at a time, mixing well after each addition. Mix in the vanilla. Reduce the speed to low and add the dry ingredients. Mix until just combined, around 5–10 seconds.

4 Add the chocolate pieces and briefly mix through without breaking them – you may have to do this by hand with a spatula.

5 Press plastic wrap on top of the dough in the bowl and refrigerate for 24–36 hours (I vote 36 hours).

6 When you're ready to bake, preheat the oven to 170°C (325°F) fan-forced. Line two baking trays with baking paper and set aside.

7 Remove half the dough from the fridge, roll the dough into golf ball-sized mounds and place onto the baking trays 2.5 cm (1 inch) apart, making sure to press in any chocolate pieces that are poking out (it will make for a more attractive cookie). Sprinkle lightly with sea salt.

8 Bake the cookies for 18–20 minutes, or until golden brown but still soft. You'll know the cookies are done when the tops turn caramel brown in colour.

9 Remove from the oven and place the baking trays on a baking rack for 10 minutes, then transfer the cookies onto another rack to cool (unless you'd prefer them warm, which is heavenly). Repeat with the remaining dough.

STORAGE

These cookies can be stored in an airtight container in a cool, dry place for up to 5 days, in the refrigerator for up to 2 weeks, or in the freezer for up to 2 months.

The dough can be refrigerated for up to 72 hours.

You can also freeze the balls in a resealable plastic bag and bake from frozen – bake for an extra 5 minutes if doing this.

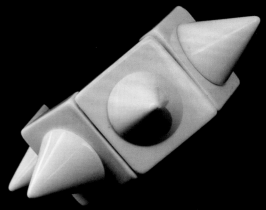

RUM CHOC COCONUT FUDGE

MAKES 20

Fudge is a classic, no-nonsense treat that is among my brother Paul's favourites. This rich, creamy confectionery has a soft, smooth texture. I love spiking my fudge recipes with a little alcohol to pack a sweet punch that isn't too overwhelming. These layered squares are addictive, so please don't eat too much fudge and drive.

350 g (12 oz) good quality dark chocolate (at least 60% cocoa), chopped

400 g (14 oz) tinned sweetened condensed milk

1 teaspoon vanilla bean paste

1½ teaspoons instant coffee

⅓ cup (80 ml) whiskey

1 tablespoon coconut oil

350 g (12 oz) good quality white chocolate, chopped

1½ teaspoons coconut extract

⅓ cup (80 ml) Malibu rum

1 cup (55 g) flaked coconut, toasted

STORAGE

This fudge can be stored in an airtight container in a cool, dry place for up to 2 weeks, in the refrigerator for 2–3 weeks, or in the freezer for up to 3 months.

1 Grease a 20 cm (8 inch) square cake tin, at least 5 cm (2 inches) deep, and line with baking paper.

2 Put the dark chocolate in a clean, dry, heatproof bowl over a saucepan of just-simmering water (the water should not touch the base of the bowl). Gently stir with a silicone spatula until melted.

3 Remove the bowl from the heat and add half the sweetened condensed milk, the vanilla bean paste, the coffee, whiskey and 2 teaspoons of the coconut oil. Stir until combined and smooth (the mixture will be thick), then spread evenly in the bottom of the tin. Place in the freezer for 30 minutes.

4 Melt the white chocolate in a clean, dry, heatproof bowl over a saucepan of just-simmering water (the water should not touch the base of the bowl). Gently stir with a silicone spatula until melted.

5 Add the remaining condensed milk and coconut oil, the coconut extract and the rum, stirring until combined. Remove the fudge from the freezer and add the white chocolate mixture on top, spreading evenly to coat. Top with the toasted coconut, then chill in the refrigerator for at least 1 hour before cutting.

6 To cut the fudge, fill a large cup with hot water. Dip a sharp knife into the water, then blot dry on paper towel. Cut the fudge into pieces.

TIP Melting chocolate in the microwave can be a great time saver. Place the chocolate in a clean, dry, microwave-safe bowl and microwave at 50% power, stirring at 30-second intervals with a silicone spatula until melted.

HUNKY CHUNKY SHORTBREAD

MAKES 16

These shortbread cookies make for an excellent gift as, not only are they utterly scrumptious, they can be packaged with minimal fuss and they travel well. They are my go-to treat when baking someone's day. The dough is shaped into logs and chilled for 2 hours, then cut into rounds and rolled in sugar. I am a big fan of using demerara sugar to add texture to baked goods, so the edge of this shortbread is my favourite part.

225 g (8 oz) unsalted butter, at room temperature, cut into 1 cm pieces

½ cup (110 g) caster (superfine) sugar

¼ cup (60 g) firmly packed soft brown sugar

1 teaspoon vanilla bean paste

2½ cups (370 g) plain (all-purpose) flour

175 g (6 oz) good quality dark chocolate (at least 70% cocoa), chopped into chunks

⅓ cup (70 g) demerara sugar, for rolling

1 large egg, beaten, chilled

1–2 pinches of sea salt flakes, for sprinkling

STORAGE

These cookies can be stored in an airtight container in a cool, dry place for up to 5 days, in the fridge for up to 2 weeks, or in the freezer for up to 2 months.

1. Line two baking trays with baking paper.

2. Using a hand-held mixer or stand mixer fitted with the paddle attachment, beat the butter, sugars and vanilla on medium–high speed until light and fluffy, around 3–5 minutes. Using a spatula, scrape down the sides of the bowl. With the mixer on low, slowly add the flour, followed by the chocolate chunks, and beat just to combine.

3. Divide the dough in half, placing each half on a large piece of plastic wrap or baking paper. Fold the plastic over so that it covers the dough to protect your hands from getting sticky. Using your hands, form the dough into a log shape; rolling it on the counter will help you smooth it out. Each log should be 5–7 cm (2–2¾ inch) diameter. Chill until totally firm, about 2 hours.

4. Preheat the oven to 175°C (345°F) fan-forced. Place a length of baking paper on your benchtop and sprinkle the demerara sugar evenly on top.

5. Brush the logs with the beaten egg then roll them in the demerara sugar.

6. Slice each log into rounds 1.5 cm (⅝ inch) thick, place them on the prepared baking trays about 2 cm (¾ inch) apart and sprinkle with a little bit of flaky salt.

7. Bake for 12–15 minutes, or until the edges are just beginning to brown. Place the trays on a baking rack and allow to cool slightly, then enjoy!

LOVE BITES

MAKES 22

The tangy fruity flavour of raspberry paired with creamy milk chocolate makes these a very moreish cookie indeed! I like to chop up a block of raspberry liquorice-studded chocolate for this recipe (Darrell Lea has a variety of different flavoured blocks found in Aussie supermarkets), but you could use any type of chocolate-covered liquorice.

180 g (6 oz) unsalted butter, at room temperature

¾ cup (165 g) caster (superfine) sugar

½ cup (110 g) firmly packed dark brown sugar

1 teaspoon vanilla bean paste

1 large egg, chilled

2⅓ cups (350 g) plain (all-purpose) flour

½ teaspoon sea salt

180 g (6 oz) milk chocolate-coated raspberry liquorice, chopped, plus a lil' extra for decorating (I like to use Darrell Lea)

100 g (3½ oz) milk chocolate, melted (for dipping once the cookies have cooled)

2 teaspoons freeze-dried raspberries (available from cake decorating stores, specialty grocers or online; optional)

1 Preheat the oven to 160°C (315°F) fan-forced. Line two baking trays with baking paper.

2 Using a hand-held mixer or a stand mixer fitted with the paddle attachment, beat the butter, caster sugar and brown sugar for 5 minutes, or until light and fluffy.

3 Add the vanilla and egg and beat until well combined. Add the flour and salt and beat until just combined. Add the chopped liquorice and beat until incorporated. Refrigerate the cookie dough for at least 30 minutes so that it firms up and is easier to handle.

4 Roll the dough into golf ball-sized mounds and place onto the trays 2 cm (¾ inches) apart.

5 Bake the cookies for 20–25 minutes, or until just golden. Leave the cookies on the trays to cool.

6 Once cooled, dip the tops of the cookies in melted milk chocolate and decorate with some extra chocolate raspberry liquorice and freeze-dried raspberries (if using).

STORAGE

These cookies can be stored in an airtight container in a cool, dry place for up to 1 week, in the refrigerator for up to 3 weeks, or in the freezer for up to 2 months.

INSTANT-HIT CARAMEL SLICE

SERVES 30

This is one of the very first recipes I learned. I adapted it from one of Mum's *Women's Weekly* cookbooks (the one all about slices). It became an instant hit with my friends – it's just so crunchy, chewy and chocolatey, and perfectly hits the spot! Feel free to add any additional toppings or flavours to make this slice uniquely yours.

BASE

1 cup (150 g) plain (all-purpose) flour, sifted

½ cup (100 g) lightly packed soft brown sugar

½ cup (45 g) desiccated coconut

¼ cup (25 g) whole rolled oats

125 g (4½ oz) unsalted butter, melted

1 Preheat the oven to 180°C (350°F) fan-forced. Grease an 18 x 28 cm (7 x 11¼ inch) slice tin, at least 5 cm (2 inches) deep, and line with baking paper.

2 Combine all the base ingredients in a bowl. Mix well, then press into the prepared tin. Bake for 15–20 minutes, or until light golden. Remove from the oven and allow to cool completely in the tin.

FILLING

800 g (1 lb 12 oz) tinned sweetened condensed milk

2 tablespoons golden syrup

60 g (2¼ oz) butter, melted

½ teaspoon vanilla bean paste

1 Combine all the filling ingredients in a medium saucepan over medium heat. Cook, whisking the bubbling mixture, for 10 minutes, or until golden. Pour the filling on top of the cooled base. Bake for 12–15 minutes, or until firm. Cool completely in the tin in the refrigerator for 3–4 hours, or until set.

TOPPING

250 g (9 oz) dark chocolate (at least 75% cocoa), chopped

2 tablespoons coconut oil

pinch sea salt flakes

1 Put the dark chocolate and oil in a clean, dry, heatproof bowl over a saucepan of just-simmering water (the water should not touch the base of the bowl). Gently stir with a silicone spatula until melted.

2 Pour the melted chocolate over the caramel filling. Refrigerate, then, as the chocolate begins to set, sprinkle with sea salt flakes. Allow to set completely before turning out and cutting with a hot knife.

TIP Melting chocolate in the microwave can be a great time saver. Place the chocolate and oil in a clean, dry, microwave-safe bowl and microwave at 50% power, stirring at 30-second intervals with a silicone spatula until melted.

STORAGE

This slice can be stored in an airtight container in a cool, dry place or in the refrigerator for up to 5 days, or in the freezer for up to 3 months.

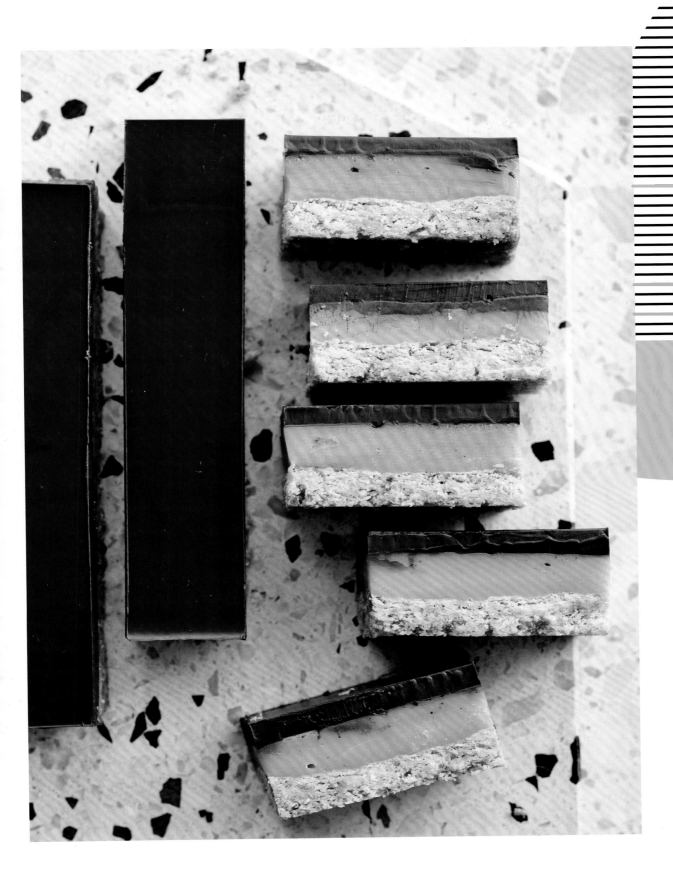

MOCHA MAGIC PINWHEELS

MAKES 40

Mocha pinwheel cookies make for an eye-catchingly graphic and tasty treat. The effect is achieved by rolling coffee-flavoured cookie dough with vanilla-flavoured cookie dough, jelly-roll style, to form the gorgeous swirl. Once baked, these cookies are nice and sturdy, making them perfect gifts to bake and take.

3 cups (450 g) plain (all-purpose) flour

1½ teaspoons baking powder

¼ teaspoon sea salt

250 g (9 oz) unsalted butter, at room temperature

1 cup (220 g) caster (superfine) sugar

1 large egg, at room temperature

1 teaspoon vanilla bean paste

1½ teaspoons instant coffee

60 g (2 oz) dark chocolate, melted and cooled slightly

STORAGE

These cookies can be stored in an airtight container in a cool, dry place for up to 5 days, in the refrigerator for up to 2 weeks, or in the freezer for up to 3 months.

1   Whisk together the flour, baking powder and salt and set aside.

2   Using a hand-held mixer or a stand mixer fitted with the paddle attachment, beat the butter on medium speed for 2–3 minutes until creamy. With the mixer on low, gradually add the sugar, then the egg and vanilla. Increase the speed to medium and beat well, then scrape down the sides and bottom of the bowl and mix again until incorporated. With the mixer on low, gradually add the flour mixture until just combined. If the dough is sticky knead in a little more flour.

3   Remove the dough from the mixer and divide into two equal portions. Return one portion to the mixer and add the instant coffee. Mix until the dough is speckled with coffee bits. Remove the coffee dough from the mixer and set aside. Return the other portion of dough to the mixer and add the melted chocolate. Mix until well combined.

4   Roll out each portion separately between two sheets of baking paper to form a 23 x 35 cm (9 x 14 inch) rectangle around 5 mm (¼ inch) thick. Transfer the pieces, still in the baking paper, to two baking trays. Chill in the refrigerator for at least 1 hour.

5   Transfer the chocolate dough onto your benchtop and remove the top layer of paper. Place the coffee dough directly on top of the chocolate dough so that they line up nicely. Gently run a rolling pin over them to press together. Let the dough stand at room temperature until malleable, around 5–10 minutes. If necessary, use a knife to trim the long side of the dough. This gives you a nice even start for the spiral. From the long side, and working slowly and carefully, roll the dough tightly, jelly-roll style, using the baking paper as a guide. The chocolate dough usually tears a little when rolling. When this happens – STOP – and pinch the dough back together before you continue to roll.

6   Cover the dough roll in baking paper, then in plastic wrap. Chill thoroughly for at least 1 hour. Turn the dough halfway through chilling to make sure it doesn't become flat on one side.

7   Preheat the oven to 170°C (325°F) fan-forced and line two baking trays with baking paper.

8   Remove the dough from the refrigerator and slice in half with a sharp knife. Place one half back in the refrigerator. Cut the other half into 5 mm (¼ inch) rounds and place them on the baking trays 2.5 cm (1 inch) apart.

9   Bake for 10–12 minutes. Let the cookies cool for 2–3 minutes on the baking trays before transferring to a baking rack. Repeat with the remaining dough.

EVERYBODY LOVES TEA CAKE

SERVES 12 🄶🄵

No fancy gimmicks or cake decorating tricks here: just pop on the kettle, cut yourself a generous slice and wait for eager friends or colleagues to arrive in record time for a morning tea treat. I used orange and ginger in this easy loaf recipe as they work so beautifully together, and a lemon cream cheese icing to balance out the sweetened spice.

CAKE

200 g (7 oz) unsalted butter, chopped into chunks

200 g (7 oz) good quality white chocolate, chopped

½ cup (110 g) firmly packed dark brown sugar

1 cup (250 ml) fresh orange juice

2 large eggs, at room temperature

1 cup (150 g) self-raising gluten-free flour

2 teaspoons cinnamon

2 teaspoons ground ginger

1½ cups (150 g) almond meal

1. Preheat your oven to 160°C (315°F) fan-forced. Grease a 13 x 23 cm (5 x 9 inch) loaf tin, 7 cm (2¾ inches) deep, and line it with baking paper.

2. Place the butter, white chocolate, sugar and orange juice in a large heavy-based saucepan. Stir the ingredients over medium–low heat with a silicone spatula for 5 minutes, or until the chocolate melts completely and the mixture is smooth. Set aside for at least 20 minutes to cool.

3. Next, add the eggs one at a time and beat in well using a hand-held mixer or whisk. Sift the flour and spices over and stir in until well combined. Next, fold in the almond meal until just combined.

4. Pour the mixture into the loaf tin and bake for 50–60 minutes, or until a wooden skewer inserted into the centre comes out almost clean. Stand the cake in the tin for at least 2 hours before turning out onto a baking rack to cool completely.

TIP You can speed up the cooling process by placing the baked cake in the refrigerator for an hour or so, covered with a clean tea towel.

LEMON CREAM CHEESE FROSTING

250 g (9 oz) cream cheese, at room temperature

75 g (2½ oz) unsalted butter, at room temperature

1 teaspoon vanilla bean paste

2 cups (250 g) icing (confectioners') sugar

1 tablespoon lemon juice

thin strands of zest from half an orange, to decorate

1. Using a hand-held mixer or a stand mixer fitted with the paddle attachment, beat the cream cheese, butter and vanilla on low speed until combined, then increase the speed to medium–high and beat until light and fluffy, about 2 minutes.

2. Add the icing sugar and the lemon juice and mix on low speed to combine. Once the sugar is mixed in, increase the speed to medium–high and beat until light and fluffy, about 1 minute.

3. Use a butter knife or an offset spatula to generously slather the frosting over the top of the cooled cake. Decorate with a scattering of orange zest.

STORAGE

This cake is best served at room temperature.

It can be made ahead and stored un-iced wrapped in plastic wrap or in an airtight container in the refrigerator for up to 5 days, or in the freezer for up to 1 month. Simply thaw it overnight in the refrigerator when ready to be used. The lemon cream cheese frosting can also be made ahead and stored in an airtight container in the refrigerator for up to 5 days, or in the freezer for up to 1 month.

LOLLY HEART COOKIES

MAKES 30

Stained-glass cookies are uniquely beautiful, so easy to make and so very festive! I love seeing light peek through the hard lolly centres and, yes, if you use a skewer to poke a hole in the top, you can decorate your Christmas tree with them. Or better still – gift them to friends and family to adorn their tree. Just try not to overcook the boiled lolly centre as it will become brittle.

1 cup hard boiled lollies (candies) in various colours

200 g (7 oz) unsalted butter, at room temperature

¾ cup (165 g) caster (superfine) sugar

2 tablespoons golden syrup or honey

2 large egg yolks, at room temperature

1 teaspoon vanilla bean paste

pinch fine salt or sea salt flakes

½ teaspoon cinnamon

3 cups (450 g) plain (all-purpose) flour

1 Divide the lollies into colour groups in separate ziplock bags. Place a tea towel over the bags and use a rolling pin or meat mallet to carefully smash the lollies until they are finely crushed.

2 Using a hand-held mixer or a stand mixer fitted with the paddle attachment, beat the butter and sugar on medium speed for 3 minutes, or until light and fluffy. Add the golden syrup or honey, egg yolks, vanilla, salt and cinnamon and beat until combined. With the mixer on low, gradually add the flour and beat to combine. Divide the dough in half, wrap each portion in plastic wrap and refrigerate for at least 30 minutes.

3 Working with one portion at a time, roll out the dough on floured baking paper to around 3 mm (¼ inch) thick. Cover with another sheet of baking paper, place on a baking tray or chopping board and refrigerate until firm, around 30 minutes. Repeat with the second portion of dough.

4 Preheat the oven to 160°C (315°F) fan-forced, and place the oven racks in the upper and lower thirds. Line two baking trays with baking paper.

5 Using a large cookie cutter (you can use a heart shape as I've done here), cut out the cookie dough. Gently re-roll and continue to cut out 'scraps', if desired. Place the cookies 2.5 cm (1 inch) apart on the trays. Then, with a smaller cookie cutter, cut out the dough in the centre of each cookie.

6 Bake for 8 minutes, or until the cookies are pale but slightly firm. Carefully remove the trays from the oven and neatly fill in the cookie centres with crushed lollies. Continue to bake for another 4 minutes, or until the cookies begin to brown at the edges and the boiled lolly centres are melted. Remove from the oven and allow the cookies to cool completely on the baking trays.

VERY STUDLY BROWNIES

**MAKES 20-25
(DEPENDING ON HOW BIG
YOU LIKE YOUR BROWNIES)**

In my opinion the best brownies contain both cocoa and melted chocolate, and butter instead of oil. What makes these my favourite brownies ever is a generous amount of dark chocolate chunks, for extra melted fudgy gloriousness to accompany the delicate crust and moist, velvety centre. These brownies are perfect to eat on their own, or you can eat them warm with a scoop of vanilla ice cream. They're the ideal companion to take to any party!

115 g (4 oz) unsalted butter

225 g (8 oz) good quality
   dark chocolate, chopped,
   plus 95 g (3¼ oz) extra

½ cup (110 g) caster
   (superfine) sugar

½ cup (100 g) lightly packed
   soft brown sugar

3 large eggs, at room temperature

½ teaspoon vanilla bean paste

½ cup (70 g) plain
   (all-purpose) flour

¼ teaspoon baking powder

1½ tablespoons Dutch
   cocoa powder

pinch sea salt

90 g (3¼ oz) good quality
   milk chocolate, chopped

⅓ cup (40 g) macadamia nuts,
   crushed and toasted

¼ cup (30 g) pecans,
   coarsely chopped

1 Preheat the oven to 170°C (325°F) fan-forced. Grease a 23 cm (9 inch) square cake tin, 5 cm (2 inches) deep, and line the base and sides with baking paper.

2 Melt the butter and 225 g (8 oz) of dark chocolate in a clean, dry, heatproof bowl over a saucepan of just-simmering water (the water should not touch the base of the bowl). Gently stir with a silicone spatula until melted. Cool for 5 minutes.

3 In a separate bowl, combine the two sugars, the eggs and vanilla and whisk by hand to combine. Pour in the butter and chocolate mixture, then sift the dry ingredients on top. Gently fold the mixture to combine.

4 Add the milk chocolate and remaining 95 g (3¼ oz) dark chocolate to the brownie mixture, then fold in the macadamia nuts and pecans.

5 Pour the mixture into the prepared tin and bake for 25 minutes, or until crusty on top and soft in the centre. Leave to cool in the tin until completely cool (unless you like eating warm brownies straight from the oven!), then turn out onto a baking rack.

6 Once cool, cut into bars to serve.

TIPS

Melting chocolate in the microwave can be a great time saver. Place the chocolate and butter in the microwave, place them in a clean, dry, microwave-safe bowl and microwave at 50% power, stirring at 30-second intervals with a silicone spatula until melted.

Brownies taste even better the next day. If you have the patience (which I tend not to), let them cool in the tin then set them aside, uncut, in an airtight container overnight.

STORAGE

These brownies can be stored in a cool, dry place in an airtight container or wrapped in two layers of foil or plastic wrap for up to 4 days, in the refrigerator for up to 1 week, or in the freezer for up to 3 months.

PASSIONFRUIT DELIGHTS

MAKES 30

This cherished recipe has been passed down through generations in my partner Troy's family (thank you Grandma Nowland!). These sweet, buttery biscuits are easy to make and even easier to eat thanks to the addition of a little rice flour, which gives a short, creamy biscuit texture. Glazed with the sweet tang of passionfruit, these cookie-jar favourites are perfect for afternoon tea.

2 teaspoons vanilla bean paste

250 g (9 oz) unsalted butter, at room temperature

⅓ cup (75 g) caster (superfine) sugar

pinch sea salt

2¼ cups (335 g) plain (all-purpose) flour, sifted

¼ cup (40 g) rice flour, sifted

1   Preheat the oven to 150°C (300°F) fan-forced, and line two baking trays with baking paper.

2   Using a hand-held mixer or a stand mixer fitted with the paddle attachment, beat the vanilla, butter, sugar and salt on medium speed for 3 minutes, or until light and fluffy.

3   Stir in the flours and press together to form a firm dough. Knead gently on a floured surface until smooth.

4   Divide the dough in half. Roll each half into a log 5 cm (2 inches) wide. Slice each log into pieces 1 cm (½ inch) thick and place onto the baking trays. Bake for 35 minutes, or until the biscuits are a pale straw colour. Transfer to a baking rack to cool before icing.

PASSIONFRUIT ICING

50 g (1¾ oz) unsalted butter, softened and cut into cubes

1 cup (125 g) icing (confectioners') sugar, sifted

1 tablespoon passionfruit pulp (with or without seeds, depending on your preference)

1   Combine the icing ingredients in a clean, dry, heatproof bowl over a saucepan of just-simmering water (the water should not touch the base of the bowl). Gently stir with a silicone spatula for 2 minutes, or until the icing is really shiny.

2   Dip each biscuit into the icing or drizzle it over the biscuits. Leave to set before serving.

STORAGE

These biscuits can be stored in an airtight container in a cool, dry place for up to 5 days.

CHRISTMAS HONEYCOMB COAL

SERVES 20

This is my rather sinister recipe for deliciously dark edible 'coal', which comes in the form of chunky, chocolate-coated honeycomb infused with cinnamon and black spiced rum. Use this novelty treat as a stocking filler for your not-so-loved ones this Christmas! If you're not a fan of rum, you can omit this ingredient completely.

1 cup (220 g) caster (superfine) sugar

¾ teaspoon smoked sea salt (but any salt is fine)

½ cup (170 g) light corn syrup or glucose syrup

1½ tablespoons black spiced rum (such as Kraken; optional)

1 teaspoon vanilla extract

½ teaspoon ground cinnamon

3 teaspoons bicarbonate of soda (baking soda)

1 Line a 23 cm (9 inch) square cake tin or baking dish, 5 cm (2 inches) deep, with foil and spray with cooking oil spray.

2 In a saucepan large enough to accommodate the mixture (which will eventually grow to 4–5 times its original size), combine the sugar, salt and corn syrup/glucose syrup and stir over low heat. Once boiling, add the black spiced rum and vanilla. Cook over medium–high heat until it reaches 'hard crack' consistency, or 145–150°C (295–300°F) on a candy thermometer. This should take around 10 minutes.

3 Remove the saucepan from the heat and immediately stir in the cinnamon and bicarbonate of soda. Take care – the mixture will bubble up significantly! Stir until just combined, being careful not to knock out the airy texture of your honeycomb. Gently and carefully pour into the prepared tray or dish.

4 Allow the honeycomb to cool completely (at least 1 hour). Once cooled, use a rolling pin to smash it into smaller chunks and be sure to remove any remaining foil.

ASSEMBLY & DECORATION

500 g (1 lb 2 oz) good quality dark chocolate, chopped

1 tablespoon coconut oil

black food colouring oil or powder

1⅓ cups (130 g) finely crushed Oreo biscuits

1 Put the dark chocolate and coconut oil in a clean, dry, heatproof bowl over a saucepan of just-simmering water (the water should not touch the base of the bowl). Gently stir with a silicone spatula until melted, then add the black food colouring until the desired shade is achieved. Mix in the crushed Oreo biscuits.

2 Line a tray with baking paper. Using a fork, dip the honeycomb pieces into the melted chocolate and transfer to the tray.

TIP Melting chocolate in the microwave can be a great time saver. Place the chocolate and coconut oil in a clean, dry, microwave-safe bowl and microwave at 50% power, stirring at 30-second intervals with a silicone spatula until melted.

STORAGE

The coal can be stored in an airtight container in a cool, dry place for up to 1 week.

'NICE BUNDT' MANDARIN CAKE

SERVES 12

During mandarin season, my mum tends to go a bit citrus crazy, buying and gifting more mandarins than anyone in our extended family could ever eat. I created this glazed bundt for an afternoon tea when my parents were visiting – I knew she'd be impressed with the zero-waste approach to baking with mandarins as the hero ingredient. Chilli adds an exciting warmth to this recipe and is perfectly complemented by the sweetness of the melted jam glaze, which keeps the cake fresh and maintains its delicious moisture.

4 mandarins

7 large eggs, at room temperature

1 cup (220 g) caster (superfine) sugar

1 cup (150 g) self-raising cake flour or self-raising flour

3½ cups (350 g) almond meal

⅓ cup (115 g) apricot jam (without pulp)

¼ teaspoon chilli powder

STORAGE

This bundt cake can be served warm, but it is just as good at room temperature. It can be stored (glazed so that it doesn't dry out) in an airtight container in the refrigerator for up to 4 days, or in the freezer for up to 1 month. Bring to room temperature to serve.

1 Place the whole mandarins (skin and all) in a large saucepan and cover with water. Bring to the boil, then reduce the heat and simmer for 1 hour. Drain the mandarins and place on a baking rack until they cool completely. Once cool, cut them open to remove any seeds, then purée the entire fruit including the skin.

2 Preheat the oven to 160°C (315°F) fan-forced. Grease a large bundt tin with cooking oil spray and lightly dust with flour (this prevents the cake from sticking to the tin once baked).

3 Using a hand-held mixer or a stand mixer fitted with the paddle attachment, beat the eggs and sugar on medium speed until fluffy, about 5 minutes.

4 Fold through the purée, flour and almond meal. Once combined, pour into the bundt tin and bake for 1 hour–1 hour 10 minutes, or until a wooden skewer inserted into the thickest part comes out clean.

5 Remove from the oven and allow to cool for 30 minutes, before turning out onto a baking rack to cool completely.

6 To make the glaze, use the stove top or microwave to gently heat the apricot jam and the chilli powder until the powder has dissolved and the mixture is runny.

7 Use a pastry brush to glaze a thin layer of melted jam all over the bundt (you can glaze the bundt cake while it is warm or once it has cooled – whatever is most convenient for you).

BELOVED PLUM CRUMBLE CAKE

SERVES 12

This is my German grandmother's most treasured recipe – a simple buttery almond cake, fresh plums and a generous topping of crispy, melt-in-your-mouth crumble. It's always fantastic taking a freshly baked, wonderfully smelling plum cake out of the oven! You can use any stone fruits to make this sumptuous bake – make use of what you can find in season.

CRUMBLE

½ cup (50 g) almond meal

⅓ cup (50 g) plain (all-purpose) flour

¼ cup (55 g) caster (superfine) sugar

50 g (1¾ oz) unsalted butter, chopped into pieces, chilled

1   Preheat the oven to 170°C (325°F) fan-forced. Grease a 22 cm (8½ inch) round cake tin (preferably with a loose bottom), 5 cm (2 inches) deep, and line the base and side with baking paper.

2   Put all the crumble ingredients in a bowl and rub together with your fingertips until crumbly, then set aside.

CAKE

175 g (6 oz) unsalted butter, at room temperature

¾ cup (165 g) caster (superfine) sugar

3 large eggs, at room temperature

1½ cups (220 g) self-raising flour, sifted

1 teaspoon baking powder, sifted

2 teaspoons vanilla extract

1 cup (100 g) almond meal

⅓ cup (85 g) sour cream

5–6 ripe plums, halved and stoned

sour cream, whipped cream or yoghurt, to serve

1   Using a hand-held mixer or a stand mixer fitted with the paddle attachment, beat the butter, sugar, eggs, flour, baking powder, vanilla, almond meal and sour cream until smooth. Pour the mixture into the cake tin and level the top. Arrange the plums, cut-side up, on top of the cake mixture, then scatter the crumble on top.

2   Bake for 1 hour 20 minutes on the middle shelf, or until a wooden skewer inserted into the centre comes out clean (the plums will remain sticky, however). Remove from the oven and allow to cool in the tin on a baking rack. Once cool, to remove the loose-bottomed tin, gently push up from the bottom using your hands or rest the cake tin base on a jar or upside-down glass in order to pop the cake upwards. Serve plain, or with sour cream, whipped cream or yoghurt.

STORAGE

This cake can be served warm or at room temperature. It can be stored in an airtight container in the refrigerator for up to 4 days, or in the freezer for up to 1 month. Bring to room temperature before serving.

CHAPTER 2

flex your spatula

Stretch your skills with these truly
impressive party starters

MAKE FRIENDS WITH MATCHA LAYER CAKE

SERVES 16-20

This light and zesty creation is perfect for friends with gluten intolerances and, in the spirit of this book, everyone deserves cake! Matcha has a uniquely earthy richness and is full of antioxidants. I combined matcha powder and fresh lemon zest in this sponge cake for depth of flavour, fragrance and a dash of the good stuff. The raspberry yoghurt cream cheese, with its sweet fruity lusciousness, cuts any bitterness and helps moisten the gluten-free crumb of the sponge.

GLUTEN-FREE LEMON & MATCHA SPONGE CAKE

165 g (5¾ oz) unsalted butter, at room temperature

1 cup (220 g) caster (superfine) sugar (you could also use coconut sugar or maple sugar)

1 teaspoon finely grated lemon zest

2 teaspoons matcha powder (available in health food stores and Asian supermarkets)

1 teaspoon vanilla extract

4 large eggs, lightly whisked, at room temperature

1½ cups (220 g) gluten-free self-raising flour

2 tablespoons hot water

1   Preheat the oven to 160°C (315°F) fan-forced. Lightly grease an 18 cm (7 inch) round cake tin, at least 8 cm (3¼ inches) deep, and line the base and side with baking paper. Ensure the baking paper creates a collar around 7.5 cm (3 inches) higher than the cake tin to allow the cake to rise.

2   Using a hand-held mixer or a stand mixer fitted with the paddle attachment, beat the butter, sugar and lemon zest on medium speed for 5 minutes, or until light, pale and creamy. Add the matcha powder and the vanilla, then the eggs, one at a time, beating well after each addition.

3   Gently fold in the flour and water until just combined — be careful not to over-mix.

4   Pour the batter into the prepared cake tin. Bake for 40–45 minutes, or until the centre of the cake springs back when lightly pressed, and a wooden skewer inserted into the centre comes out clean. Remove from the oven and allow to cool for 15–20 minutes before turning out onto a baking rack to cool completely. Once cooled, use a cake leveller or a long, thin knife, to carefully divide the cake into three even layers. Cover and set aside until assembly.

TIP   I cool my sponge cake upside-down to create a flat top that doesn't need trimming.

RASPBERRY YOGHURT CREAM CHEESE

500 g (1 lb 2 oz) cream cheese,
at room temperature

3 tablespoons Greek yoghurt

1 teaspoon vanilla bean paste

1 cup (125 g) icing (confectioners')
sugar, sifted

40 g (1½ oz) freeze-dried
raspberry powder (available
from cake decorating stores,
specialty grocers or online)

3–4 drops natural pink food
colouring (optional)

1 Using a hand-held mixer or a stand mixer fitted with the paddle attachment, beat the cream cheese, yoghurt and vanilla on high speed for 3 minutes, or until light and fluffy. Add the icing sugar and gently beat until incorporated. Add the raspberry powder and beat until fluffy. If using natural pink colouring, tint until the desired colour is achieved. You may need to chill the mixture in the refrigerator for 10–20 minutes or until thickened and more workable for piping in between the cake layers.

TIP To avoid an icing-sugar explosion, I turn the mixer off to add the icing sugar and then slowly turn it back up to full speed to incorporate it.

ASSEMBLY & DECORATION

large piping bag fitted with
a 2 cm (¾ inch) round nozzle

½ cup (175 g) lemon curd
(homemade is always best – see
p. 226, but store-bought is just
fine! Whatever makes you happy)

1½ cups (185 g) fresh raspberries

handful of edible flowers (available
from specialty grocers and online)

2 tablespoons icing sugar, to dust

1 Working on a cake turntable, secure the bottom layer of cake onto a cake board with a small dollop of raspberry yoghurt cream cheese and then gently twist in place.

2 Fill the piping bag with raspberry yoghurt cream cheese and, working from the outside in, pipe dollops onto the cake. Use a teaspoon to dollop lemon curd in between the cream cheese filling. Top with 6–8 raspberries.

3 Place the second layer of cake on top and gently press down to secure. Repeat adding the filling and chill again if needed.

4 Place the third and final layer of cake on top and gently press down to secure. Repeat adding the filling.

5 Using the photo as a guide, artfully decorate your cake with raspberries, edible flowers and a light dusting of icing sugar. ENJOY!

TIP No time to pipe? No worries! Feel free to dollop with a spoon or spread the cream cheese filling straight onto your cake layers.

STORAGE

This cake is best served at room temperature. It can be stored in an airtight container in the refrigerator for up to 3 days.

'THANK YOU OMA' BLACK FOREST CAKE

SERVES 24

My German grandmother, Liselotte, taught me how to bake (and most importantly, to bake with love) when I was a little girl. She would always have a beautifully presented crumble cake or plum tart ready for my younger brother, Paul, and me whenever we came to visit. Before migrating to Australia after WWII, Grandma was from the Black Forest, a large forested mountain range in south-west Germany. Coincidentally, she loved a heartily home-made Black Forest cake – especially when paired with a good cherry brandy. Here is her (and my) favourite version of a Black Forest cake.

CHOC-HEAVEN CAKE

3 cups (450 g) self-raising flour

2½ cups (550 g) caster (superfine) sugar

1½ cups (160 g) Dutch cocoa powder

1 teaspoon bicarbonate of soda (baking soda)

½ teaspoon sea salt

1 teaspoon instant coffee

1½ cups (375 ml) buttermilk, at room temperature

¾ cup (170 g) coconut oil, melted

3 large eggs, at room temperature

2 teaspoons vanilla extract

1½ cups (375 ml) boiling water

1 Preheat the oven to 160°C (315°F) fan-forced. Grease three 18 cm (7 inch) round cake tins, at least 5 cm (2 inches) deep, with cooking oil spray and line with baking paper.

2 Using a hand-held mixer or a stand mixer fitted with the paddle attachment, beat the flour, sugar, cocoa, bicarbonate of soda, salt and instant coffee until combined.

3 Add the buttermilk, coconut oil, eggs and vanilla and beat on medium speed until well combined. Reduce the speed, carefully add the boiling water and beat until well combined.

4 Divide the batter evenly between the tins. Bake for 45–50 minutes, or until a wooden skewer inserted into the centre comes out clean. Remove from the oven and allow to cool for 20 minutes, before turning out onto a baking rack to cool completely.

ASSEMBLY & DECORATION

cherry brandy (such as Kirsch),
to splash between the
cake layers (optional)

2½ cups (625 ml) thick
(double) cream, whipped

½ cup (165 g) cherry jam
(berry jams are also fine!)

300 g (10½ oz) cherries,
halved with pips removed

60 g (2¼ oz) block of your favourite
chocolate, shaved on the longest
edge with a vegetable peeler
or grater to create pretty curls

15 cherries, some dusted in edible
gold powder if you like (available
from cake decorating stores)

edible gold leaf (available from
cake decorating stores; optional)

1   Place one cake onto a cake stand or serving platter and freely
splash with cherry brandy, or apply with a pastry brush – depending
on how much you enjoy kirsch! Generously spread this bottom layer
with some whipped cream, followed by some dollops of jam. Poke
some halved cherries into the filling. Repeat with the remaining two
cakes and remaining filling.

2   Cover the top layer of cream with chocolate curls: Finish with whole
cherries (dusted in gold if you like, for a real show-stopping effect)
and some edible gold leaf, if using.

ROSE & FIG LOVE CAKES

SERVES 8

It is almost impossible to resist becoming enchanted with these beautiful mini love cakes. The delicate flavour of rosewater and the tanginess of the cream cheese is complemented by the satisfying crunch of crushed pistachios. Adorned with sweet, plump, gold-kissed figs and jewel-like cubes of Turkish delight, these mini cakes are sure to win hearts! The use of almond meal and dark brown sugar lends a lovely sticky, rich profile that can't be achieved with just flour, butter and eggs alone.

SPICED CARAMEL & ALMOND MINI LOAVES

200 g (7 oz) unsalted butter, chopped into chunks

200 g (7 oz) good quality white chocolate, chopped

⅔ cup (150 g) firmly packed dark brown sugar

1 cup (250 ml) hot water

2 tablespoons honey or golden syrup

2 teaspoons vanilla extract

2 large eggs, at room temperature

1 cup (150 g) self-raising cake flour or self-raising flour

2 teaspoons cinnamon

1 teaspoon ground ginger

1 teaspoon ground cardamom

2 cups (200 g) almond meal

1 Preheat the oven to 160°C (315°F) fan-forced. Grease the holes of an 8-capacity (230 ml/7¾ fl oz) mini loaf tin and line the base and sides of each cavity with baking paper.

2 Place the butter, chocolate, sugar, water, honey or golden syrup and vanilla into a large heavy-based saucepan. Stir the ingredients over medium–low heat with a silicone spatula for 5 minutes, or until the chocolate melts completely and the mixture is smooth. Set aside for at least 20 minutes to cool, then transfer to a mixing bowl.

3 Add the eggs to the chocolate mixture one at a time, and beat in well using a hand-held mixer or whisk. Sift in the flour and spices and mix until well combined. Fold in the almond meal until well combined.

4 Fill each cavity to three-quarters full. Bake for 30 minutes, or until a wooden skewer inserted into the centre comes out clean. Leave in the tin to cool completely.

TIP You can speed up the process of cooling your cakes by placing the whole tray in the refrigerator, covered with a clean tea towel, for an hour or so.

ROSE CREAM CHEESE

500 g (1 lb 2 oz) cream cheese,
  at room temperature

100 g (3½ oz) unsalted butter,
  chopped, at room temperature

1 cup (125 g) icing (confectioners')
  sugar, sifted

½ teaspoon rosewater

2 teaspoons lemon juice

3–4 drops pink food colouring

⅔ cup (170 ml) thick (double)
  cream, whipped

1 Using a hand-held mixer or a stand mixer fitted with the paddle attachment, beat the cream cheese, butter, icing sugar, rosewater and lemon juice on high for 2–3 minutes, or until pale and fluffy.

2 Add the food colouring until the desired colour is achieved, stirring to combine thoroughly.

3 Gently fold in the whipped cream until combined and then cover and set aside until needed.

TIP If your filling appears to be too soft to pipe neatly onto your cakes, place it in the refrigerator for 20–30 minutes to firm up to a more workable consistency.

ASSEMBLY & DECORATION

large piping bag lined
  with a star nozzle

1 cup (130 g) crushed pistachios

40 g (1½ oz) Turkish delight,
  chopped into small cubes

3 fresh figs, sliced into wedges

edible gold leaf (available from
  cake decorating stores; optional)

1 Pipe the rose cream cheese in swirls onto each mini loaf. Adorn each cake with crushed pistachios, a scattering of Turkish delight cubes and segments of fresh fig.

2 If you like, add a decadent lustre to the topping by decorating with a scattering of gold leaf.

STORAGE

These cakes are best served at room temperature. They can be stored in an airtight container in the refrigerator for up to 4 days. It's best to bring them back to room temperature before serving, but straight from the fridge is yummy too.

DEATH BY CHOC CHEESECAKE

SERVES 24

Hit the spot with this heavenly rich chocolate hazelnut cheesecake. It's a real crowd-pleaser and sure to win over your colleagues at morning tea (I used this trick during my time as a high school teacher and, yes, it works). You can make this recipe ahead of time because it freezes beautifully. While this cheesecake doesn't take long to put together, it does need ample time to chill before adding the decadent topping. Because of its rich denseness, a little goes a long way!

CRUST

250 g (9 oz) chocolate biscuits (see Tip)

60 g (2 oz) chopped hazelnuts

125 g (4½ oz) unsalted butter, melted

¼ teaspoon sea salt

1 Preheat the oven to 160°C (315°F) fan-forced. Grease and line a 25 cm (10 inch) springform tin.

2 Place the chocolate biscuits and chopped hazelnuts in the bowl of a food processor. Pulse them to fine crumbs. Transfer to a large mixing bowl and add the melted butter and salt. Mix together and press into the bottom of the tin. Bake for 10 minutes. Remove from the oven and allow to cool in the tin on a baking rack for around 30 minutes.

TIP Any plain chocolate biscuits can be used to make the crust; I used Arnott's Chocolate Ripple biscuits in this recipe.

FILLING

340 g (12 oz) good quality dark chocolate, chopped

1 kg (2 lb 4 oz) cream cheese, at room temperature

2 cups (440 g) caster (superfine) sugar

4 large eggs, at room temperature

1 tablespoon Dutch cocoa powder

1 tablespoon hazelnut liqueur or 2 teaspoons vanilla extract

2 cups (490 g) sour cream, at room temperature

1 Place the chocolate in a clean, dry, microwave-safe bowl and microwave at 50% power, stirring at 30-second intervals with a silicone spatula until melted. Set aside.

2 Using a hand-held mixer or a stand mixer fitted with the paddle attachment, beat the cream cheese on medium speed until smooth. Gradually beat in the sugar until well blended. Add the eggs one at a time, beating on low speed after each addition until blended. Add the melted chocolate, cocoa powder and hazelnut liqueur (or vanilla). Beat on low speed until combined. Add the sour cream and stir together with a large silicone spatula. Pour onto the prepared crust in the tin.

3 Bake for 1 hour 20 minutes, or until the cheesecake is set at the edges with just a slight wobble in the centre. Remove from the oven and allow to cool completely in the tin. Refrigerate until firm, about 4 hours, or overnight.

4 Run a small knife between the cheesecake and springform tin to loosen the collar, then remove the collar.

TOPPINGS

¾ cup (225 g) chocolate
hazelnut spread, such as
Nutella, plus 2 tablespoons
extra, heated until runny

¾ cup (185 ml) thick (double)
cream, whipped to stiff peaks

60 g (2¼ oz) block of your favourite
chocolate, shaved on the longest
edge with a vegetable peeler
or grater to create pretty curls

Just before serving, top the cheesecake with heaped spoonfuls of
the chocolate hazelnut spread, whipped cream and the chocolate
shavings. Drizzle with the additional warmed chocolate hazelnut
spread for some extra decadence!

STORAGE

If there are leftovers, slice into portions before refrigerating.
This cheesecake can be stored in an airtight container in the
refrigerator for up to 5 days.

To make ahead and freeze, chill the baked cheesecake
for 4 hours, or until firm. Do not apply the toppings; most
chocolate hazelnut spreads will firm up in the refrigerator,
making the cheesecake difficult to slice neatly. Wrap in two
layers of plastic wrap and then place in the freezer. Thaw in
the refrigerator for 24 hours before serving. Apply the spread,
whipped cream and shavings just before serving.

SUMMER DAYS BANOFFEE PIE

SERVES 8-10

Banoffee pie is one of my favourite indulgences and this summery version is an impressive way to bake someone's day (you'll need to plan ahead though because this pie needs to freeze for 4-6 hours). Layers of milk caramel, whipped banana cream, nuts and shaved chocolate atop a buttery biscuit crust make this banoffee pie the ultimate dessert temptation for a hot day! Find the ripest bananas you can get your hands on for the creamy semifreddo, as they help sweeten the filling.

CRUST

2 cups (200 g) graham cracker crumbs

115 g (4 oz) unsalted butter, melted

In a large bowl, combine the graham cracker crumbs and butter and stir until the crumbs are well coated with the butter and the mixture resembles wet sand. Grease a 23 cm (9 inch) loose-bottomed pie dish, at least 5 cm (2 inches) deep, and press the crumb mixture into the bottom and up the side. Freeze until firm, about 25 minutes.

TIP If you can't find graham crackers you can use plain digestives or Arnott's Nice biscuits as a substitute.

FILLING

3 large very ripe bananas

1 tablespoon fresh lemon juice

2 cups (500 ml) thick (double) cream, whipped to firm peaks

1 teaspoon vanilla bean paste

Meanwhile, in a large bowl, mash together the bananas with the lemon juice using a fork or potato masher. When the mixture is smooth, fold in the whipped cream and vanilla. Mix until the mashed bananas are well dispersed throughout the cream.

TIP I recommend taste-testing here. The mixture should be lightly sweet if you've used very ripe bananas. If you find the mixture is not sweet enough – or if you used under-ripe bananas – fold in 2–3 tablespoons of icing (confectioners') sugar, to taste. Note that this filling will be layered with very sweet dulce de leche, so you may want to be sparing with the extra sugar.

ASSEMBLY & DECORATION

½ cup (75 g) hazelnuts

380 g (13½ oz) dulce de leche
(see p. 229, or use store-bought)

piping bag fitted with a 5 mm
(¼ inch) round nozzle

60 g (2¼ oz) block of your
favourite dark chocolate,
shaved on the longest edge
with a vegetable peeler or
grater to create pretty curls

(see p. 229, or use store-bought)

STORAGE

This semifreddo banoffee
pie can be tightly wrapped in
plastic wrap and stored in an
airtight container in the freezer
for up to 1 month.

1 Preheat the oven to 160°C (315°F) fan-forced. Roughly chop the hazelnuts and place them in a single layer on a baking tray. Roast for 5–10 minutes, or until lightly golden. Set aside to cool.

2 Remove the pie crust from the freezer and spread half of the dulce de leche evenly over the crust. Top with the whipped banana mixture. Transfer the remaining dulce de leche to a microwave-safe bowl and heat for 30 seconds at 100% power to make it easier to pipe. Stir well, transfer the caramel to the piping bag and pipe chubby kisses around the middle (as pictured). Garnish with the roasted hazelnuts and shaved chocolate.

3 Freeze the pie uncovered for 2 hours. Cover with plastic wrap and freeze for an additional 4 hours or overnight before serving.

4 When you're ready to serve the pie, use a large chef's knife dipped in hot water and wiped dry to cut into slices. I find that leaving the pie to stand for 5–7 minutes at room temperature makes it soft enough to slice without much resistance.

STICKY GINGER MAGIC FLAN CAKE

SERVES 12

This deliciously rich Latin layered dessert is the kind of cake that makes you close your eyes after you taste it, because the contrasting creamy, cakey, pudding-like textures are glorious. The 'magic' part of this cake takes place in the oven. The gingery cake batter is poured into the tin first and then the flan mixture is poured on top. During the baking process, the two switch places!

There are two important things to know about this recipe: you'll need to start it one day ahead, as the cake needs to chill in the fridge for 8 hours (or overnight); and the cake is cooked in a water bath, which sounds complicated but is actually very easy.

This cake is best served at home where you can unmould it at the table and let your friends watch the flowing caramel topping cascade down the side of the cake – it's sure to impress close friends who think they've seen it all and the extra effort in this recipe is sure to make your guests feel special.

....

CAKE

- 155 g (5½ oz) salted caramel (see p. 228, but store-bought is fine too)
- ⅔ cup (100 g) plain (all-purpose) flour
- 2 teaspoons ground ginger
- 2 teaspoons cinnamon
- ½ teaspoon bicarbonate of soda (baking soda)
- ¼ teaspoon sea salt
- 220 g (7¾ oz) white chocolate, chopped
- 85 g (3 oz) unsalted butter, at room temperature
- ½ cup (125 ml) buttermilk, at room temperature
- ½ cup (110 g) caster (superfine) sugar
- 2 large eggs, at room temperature
- 1 teaspoon vanilla extract

1 Preheat the oven to 180°C (350°F) fan-forced. Grease a 12-cup (26 x 9 cm/10½ x 3½ inch) bundt tin with cooking oil spray. Pour the salted caramel evenly into the bottom of the tin.

2 In a medium bowl, sift together the flour, ginger, cinnamon, bicarbonate of soda and salt, then set aside.

3 Place the chocolate and butter in a clean, dry, microwave-safe bowl and microwave at 50% power, stirring at 30-second intervals with a silicone spatula, until smooth.

4 Add the buttermilk, sugar, eggs and vanilla to the melted chocolate mixture and whisk until incorporated. Add the flour mixture and stir until combined. Pour the chocolate batter evenly over the caramel in the tin. Set aside.

FLAN

800 g (1 lb 12 oz) tinned sweetened condensed milk

2½ cups (625 ml) full-cream milk, at room temperature

175 g (6 oz) cream cheese, at room temperature

6 large eggs, at room temperature

4 large egg yolks, at room temperature

1 teaspoon vanilla bean paste (vanilla extract is fine too)

1 Add all the flan ingredients to a blender and process on 'liquefy' (high) until smooth. Slowly pour the flan mixture over the cake batter.

2 Place the cake tin in a large roasting pan and then place it in the oven. Fill a small jug with hot water from the tap, then carefully pour water into the roasting pan until it reaches halfway up the sides of the bundt tin. Bake the cake for 1 hour 20 minutes–1 hour 40 minutes, or until a wooden skewer inserted into the centre comes out with a few moist crumbs clinging. Gently remove the bundt tin from the roasting pan and place it on a baking rack to cool completely in the tin. Refrigerate the cake in the pan for 8 hours, or overnight.

3 To unmould the cake, fill a large bowl (or your sink) with hot water. Place the bottom of the cake tin in the water to warm the caramel/flan portion of the cake. This will help to release the cake. Turn the cake out onto a large serving platter or a cake stand that has a lip. The caramel will drizzle down over the cake as you remove the tin. Serve immediately.

STRAWBERRY JELLY PANNA COTTA TART

SERVES 16

Panna cotta is a delicate and elegant dessert, and this retro-inspired tart reiteration featuring a wobbly layer of strawberry jelly and crumbly biscuit texture gives it a little more personality. All the elements of this recipe are relatively simple and straightforward, but you will need some time and patience waiting for the strawberry jelly and panna cotta layers to set. This tart is a welcome guest at any summer picnic.

BISCUIT CRUST

400 g (14 oz) of your favourite semi-sweet biscuits (I used half Shredded Wheatmeal biscuits and half Butternut Snap biscuits)

100 g (3½ oz) unsalted butter, melted

100 g (3½ oz) good quality white chocolate, melted with 3 tablespoons vegetable oil

1   Grease a 25 cm (10 inch) tart tin with a removable base, at least 6 cm (2½ inches) deep. Place the biscuits in a food processor and process until fine crumbs form. Add the melted butter and pulse until well combined (the mixture should clump together when squeezed with your fingers).

2   Place the mixture into the tart tin. Using your fingers or the back of a metal soup spoon, evenly press the mix into the bottom and up the side of the tin. Place the tart tin on a tray and leave to chill in the refrigerator for at least 30 minutes.

3   Using a pastry brush, apply a coat of melted white chocolate evenly over the inside of your tart shell. This will set quickly and acts as a shield against moisture – keeping your tart shell nice and crunchy!

STRAWBERRY JELLY & PANNA COTTA FILLING

½ sachet (40 g) strawberry jelly crystals (this should make 1 cup/250 ml; I used Aeroplane Jelly brand)

1 cup (150 g) strawberries, hulled and sliced

1 vanilla bean, split, with seeds scraped, or 1 teaspoon vanilla bean paste

⅓ cup (90 g) caster (superfine) sugar

3 cups (750 ml) thick (double) cream

6 titanium-strength gelatine leaves

1   Prepare the strawberry jelly as per the packet instructions. Allow it to cool to room temperature before slowly pouring the runny, lukewarm jelly into the tart shell. Scatter the sliced strawberries over the jelly. Leave the jelly to chill in the refrigerator for at least 1 hour, or until the jelly has firmed.

2   To make the panna cotta layer, place the vanilla pod and seeds in a small saucepan with the sugar and half of the cream. Bring to a simmer over low heat. As soon as it comes to a simmer remove it from the heat.

3   Meanwhile, soak the gelatine leaves in cold water for 5 minutes to soften them. Remove the gelatine leaves and squeeze out any excess water. Add these to the warm cream mixture and stir to dissolve. Set aside to cool.

4   Whip the remaining cream until soft peaks form, then gently fold this into the cooled vanilla cream. Pour the mixture into the tart shell and level by gently spinning or tapping the tin on the counter top. Chill in the refrigerator for at least 2 hours, or until firm.

ASSEMBLY & DECORATION

1 cup (125 g) fresh raspberries

1 cup (150 g) strawberries,
  hulled and sliced

a few small basil or mint
  leaves (optional)

2 teaspoons freeze-dried
  raspberries or strawberries,
  (available from cake decorating
  stores, specialty grocers
  or online; optional)

½ cup (175 g) honey
  or pure maple syrup

Carefully remove the tart from the tin by gently easing it up from the base. Place it on your favourite serving plate and adorn with raspberries, strawberries and basil leaves (if using). If you like, use your fingers to crumble the freeze-dried berries over the top. For a little bit of extra sweetness, drizzle with honey or maple syrup.

ESPRESSO BISCOFF INDULGENCE

SERVES 20-24

Biscoff cookies are like delicate shortbread cookies packed with dessert spices (cinnamon, nutmeg, ginger, to name a few) and are deep-buttery caramel in flavour. My German grandmother always had a jar of these at the ready in her pantry for afternoon tea. Crisp buttery Biscoff cookies dunked in strong coffee is a favourite flavour combination of mine, and it's the inspiration for this cake. Espresso cake layers are filled with Biscoff buttercream and the entire cake is frosted with an irresistible mocha Biscoff frosting.

. . . .

ESPRESSO CAKE

2¼ cups (335 g) plain (all-purpose) flour

1 teaspoon bicarbonate of soda (baking soda)

½ teaspoon sea salt

¼ cup (60 ml) hot water

2 tablespoons instant coffee

1 cup (220 g) caster (superfine) sugar

¼ cup (60 g) firmly packed soft brown sugar

125 g (4½ oz) unsalted butter, at room temperature

3 large eggs, at room temperature

1 teaspoon vanilla extract

1 cup (250 ml) buttermilk, at room temperature

1   Preheat the oven to 170°C (325°F) fan-forced. Grease four 18 cm (7 inch) single layer cake tins, at least 5 cm (2 inches) deep, and line the bases with baking paper.

2   Sift the flour, bicarbonate of soda and salt into a large bowl, then set aside.

3   Combine the water and instant coffee in a small bowl or cup and allow to cool slightly.

4   Whisk together the caster sugar and brown sugar in a small bowl.

5   Using a hand-held mixer or a stand mixer fitted with the paddle attachment, beat ¼ cup of the sugar mixture with the softened butter until well incorporated. Add the rest of the sugar ¼ cup at a time, beating well with each addition. Add the coffee mixture and blend well. Add the eggs, one at a time, and then the vanilla. Add the flour mixture, alternating with the buttermilk, beginning and ending with the flour.

6   Divide the batter evenly between the tins and bake for 20 minutes, or until a wooden skewer inserted in the centre comes out clean. Remove from the oven and allow to cool for 10 minutes, before turning out onto a baking rack to cool.

. . . .

BISCOFF FILLING

255 g (9 oz) Biscoff spread or other cookie butter spread

2 cups (250 g) icing (confectioners') sugar

125 g (4½ oz) unsalted butter, at room temperature

3 tablespoons thick (double) cream

1   Using a hand-held mixer or stand mixer fitted with the paddle attachment, beat all the ingredients except the cream until well incorporated. If the mixture is dry, add cream, 1 tablespoon at a time, until a smooth consistency is achieved. The mixture should be thick but spreadable.

MOCHA-BISCOFF BUTTERCREAM

250 g (9 oz) unsalted
  butter, softened to a
  spreadable consistency

65 g (2¼ oz) Biscoff spread or
  other cookie butter spread

2 cups (250 g) icing
  (confectioners') sugar

2 teaspoons instant coffee

2 tablespoons Dutch cocoa powder

I   Using a hand-held mixer or stand mixer fitted with the paddle attachment, beat the softened butter, Biscoff spread and icing sugar until well combined. Add the instant coffee and cocoa powder and beat again until well combined. Scrape down the sides of the bowl and beat on high speed for 2–3 minutes, or until light and fluffy. Set aside until needed.

ASSEMBLY & DECORATION

medium–large piping bag
  fitted with a 1 cm (½ inch)
  tear-shaped (ruffling) piping tip

3 tablespoons crisp pearls
  (chocolate-coated cereal
  decorations available from
  cake decorating stores)

3 Biscoff biscuits, crushed

I   Secure the bottom layer of cake onto a cake board with a small dollop of mocha-Biscoff buttercream and gently twist in place. Use an offset spatula to spread a 5 mm (¼ inch) layer of Biscoff filling right to the edge of the cake.

2   Repeat this process until you have used all the cake layers, leaving the final top layer uncovered.

3   Place the mocha-Biscoff buttercream into a piping bag fitted with a tear-shaped nozzle and decorate the top of the cake with buttercream ruffles. Top with crisp pearls and crushed Biscoff biscuits.

STORAGE

This cake is best enjoyed at room temperature, but it will last for up to 4 days when stored refrigerated in an airtight container or plastic wrap.

The espresso cake can be made 1–2 days in advance and kept in an airtight container until ready to use.

VERY VEGAN CARAMEL SLICE

MAKES 16-20

Some of my mates are vegan or lactose intolerant, so I wanted to create a version of everyone's favourite treat that they could enjoy. While I always believe in options, there is no substitute for the tinned sweetened condensed coconut milk in this recipe – replacing it may change the structure of the caramel and cause it to curdle.

CHEWY SHORTBREAD BASE

2 cups (300 g) plain (all-purpose) flour

½ cup (45 g) desiccated coconut

⅔ cup (150 g) vegan butter or margarine

½ cup (60 g) icing (confectioners') sugar

pinch sea salt

1   Preheat the oven to 180°C (350°F) fan-forced. Grease a 20 cm (8 inch) square cake tin, 6 cm (2½ inches) deep, and line with baking paper so that the paper creates a collar around 5 cm (2 inches) higher than the cake tin – this will help you lift the slice out later.

2   Add all the ingredients and 1 tablespoon water to a food processor and blitz until combined. The mixture should stick together when it is pinched between two fingers. Add a little more water if the mixture is too crumbly or more flour if it's too soft.

3   Firmly press the base mixture into the tin. Bake for 10 minutes, or until slightly golden.

CARAMEL FILLING

640 g (1 lb 7 oz) tinned sweetened condensed coconut milk

280 g (10 oz) vegan butter or margarine

½ cup (110 g) firmly packed dark brown sugar

2 teaspoons rice malt syrup

1 teaspoon vanilla bean paste

1   Place all the ingredients into a saucepan and heat over medium–high heat. Simmer, stirring constantly, for 15 minutes, or until the caramel is a deep golden brown colour and has reached 120°C (235°F) on a candy thermometer. If you are unsure, just cook the caramel until thickened and whisk to emulsify any split oil back into the caramel.

2   Pour the caramel into the tin and set aside in the refrigerator for at least 2 hours, or until the caramel is firm to the touch.

CHOCOLATE TOPPING

210 g (7½ oz) vegan chocolate, roughly chopped

3 tablespoons (45 g) coconut oil, melted, or unflavoured vegetable oil

1   Put the chocolate and coconut oil in a clean, dry, heatproof bowl over a saucepan of just-simmering water (the water should not touch the base of the bowl). Gently stir with a silicone spatula until melted. Pour the melted chocolate on top of the caramel layer and return the slice to the refrigerator to set.

2   To serve, pull the baking paper up to remove the slice from the tin. Use a sharp knife to cut it into squares or rectangles.

STORAGE

This slice can be stored refrigerated in an airtight container for up to 2 weeks or in the freezer for up to 1 month.

CHOC-ON-CHOC TART

SERVES 20-24

This is an invigoratingly rich vegan tart for all the TRUE chocolate lovers out there. Chocolate is my most favourite food group and this decadent creation is as close as I can get to the good stuff without injecting it directly into my veins (no, please don't do that). Cayenne pepper adds 'warmth' and intensifies the flavour of the dark chocolate filling, rather than adding spiciness to this dessert. I finish it off with some edible gold leaf to elevate this treat to heavenly heights.

CHOC-COCONUT & ALMOND CRUST

4 cups (400 g) almond meal

1 cup (105 g) raw cacao powder (deeper in taste than cocoa powder but, for this recipe, these ingredients are interchangeable)

¼ cup (45 g) cacao nibs

½ cup (125 ml) coconut oil, melted

¾ cup (185 ml) pure maple syrup or any natural syrup (such as rice malt syrup or coconut nectar), to taste

50 g (1¾ oz) good quality vegan dark chocolate (70% cocoa), melted

1. Preheat the oven to 160°C (315°F) fan-forced. Grease a 25 cm (10 inch) tart tin with a removable bottom, at least 6 cm (2½ inches) deep.

2. Using a hand-held mixer or stand mixer fitted with the paddle attachment, mix the almond meal, raw cacao powder, cacao nibs, coconut oil and maple syrup in short bursts until a dough forms (the dough should clump together when squeezed with your fingers).

3. Transfer the dough to the prepared tin. Using your fingers or the back of a metal soup spoon, evenly press the dough into the bottom and up the side of the tin.

4. Bake for approximately 15–20 minutes, or until the crust has firmed. Stand the tin on a baking rack and allow to cool completely, or for at least 1 hour.

5. Using a pastry brush, apply a coat of melted chocolate evenly over the inside of the tart shell. Once set, the chocolate will act as a shield against moisture, keeping your tart shell nice and crispy!

DARK CHOCOLATE & COCONUT FUDGE FILLING

400 g (14 oz) good quality vegan dark chocolate (70% cocoa), finely chopped

400 ml (14 fl oz) tinned coconut cream

2 teaspoons vanilla extract

⅓ teaspoon cayenne or chilli powder (don't fret! – this adds 'warmth' and intensifies the flavour of the filling, rather than adding spiciness)

pinch sea salt flakes

100 ml (3½ fl oz) pure maple syrup or any natural syrup, to taste

1 Place the chopped chocolate in a large mixing bowl. In a small saucepan, bring the coconut cream, vanilla extract and cayenne powder to a boil. Carefully pour the hot coconut cream mixture over the chocolate and let stand for 1 minute, then whisk until smooth and creamy. Once combined, mix in a tiny amount of sea salt flakes. Add maple syrup, to taste. Allow to cool until thickened and no longer hot to the touch.

2 Pour the fudge filling into the cooled tart shell. Now gently spin the tart tin or tap on the outer rim of the tin to level the top of the filling. Place in the refrigerator and chill for at least 2 hours, or until set.

ASSEMBLY & DECORATION

edible gold leaf (available in cake decorating stores)

1 To remove the tart from the loose-bottomed tin, gently push up from the bottom using your hands, or rest the tart tin base on a jar or upside-down glass in order to pop the tart upwards.

2 Use a clean dry brush to gently apply the gold leaf.

STORAGE

This tart can be served either chilled or at room temperature. It can be stored in an airtight container in a cool, dry place for up to 3 days, in the refrigerator for 5 days or in the freezer for up to 1 month (let it thaw overnight in the refrigerator).

STICKY CHOC CAKENUTS

MAKES 12 LARGE OR 15 SMALL DONUTS **V**

These cakenuts are just as visually appealing and fun as regular donuts, but without the added hassle and mess of frying in oil. Moist, dense and dark, they are everything a chocolate lover could want, and they just so happen to be vegan, too! You can find donut baking trays in most cake decorating stores, department stores and online. I use mine all the time, and especially when prepping for parties.

CAKE

1⅓ cups (200 g) plain (all-purpose) flour

2 teaspoons baking powder

pinch sea salt flakes

⅔ cup (150 g) firmly packed dark brown sugar

¾ cup (185 ml) vegan milk (such as soy or coconut milk)

2 tablespoons (40 g) unsweetened coconut yogurt

50 g (1¾ oz) vegan butter

70 g (2½ oz) vegan dark chocolate

1 Preheat the oven to 170°C (325°F) fan-forced. Lightly spray a six-hole donut tray with cooking oil spray.

2 Whisk the flour, baking powder, salt and sugar together in a large mixing bowl.

3 Place the wet ingredients and chocolate in a clean, dry, heatproof bowl over a saucepan of just-simmering water (the water should not touch the base of the bowl). Gently stir with a silicone spatula until melted. Allow to cool.

4 Add the wet mixture to the dry and whisk to combine, being careful not to over-mix. Transfer the batter to the donut holes with a spoon or piping bag. Bake for 15 minutes, or until the donuts spring back when gently pressed.

5 Remove the donuts from the oven and let them cool in the tray for a few minutes before turning them out onto a baking rack. Allow to cool completely before glazing. When the donut tray is cool, grease it again and cook the remaining donut batter.

TIP Melting chocolate in the microwave can be a great time saver. Place the wet ingredients and chocolate in a clean, dry, microwave-safe bowl and microwave at 50% power, stirring at 30-second intervals with a silicone spatula until melted.

CHOCOLATE GLAZE

85 g (3 oz) vegan dark chocolate, chopped, plus 50 g (1¾ oz) extra, grated, to decorate

1 tablespoon coconut oil

25 g (1 oz) vegan butter

1 Melt the chopped chocolate, coconut oil and butter using the double-boiler or microwave method described above until smooth.

2 Dip the tops of the donuts into the chocolate glaze, sprinkle with the grated chocolate and place on a baking rack to set.

STORAGE

These chocolate cakenuts are best enjoyed at room temperature to maintain their moisture. They can be stored in an airtight container in a cool, dry place for up to 2 days or in the refrigerator for up to 3 days.

LEMON TARTLET KISSES

MAKES 30

These beautiful bite-sized flavour bombs are my go-to for picnics, parties and even wedding celebrations. For ultimate convenience, this recipe uses pre-made mini tart shells; there are so many good ones available now that you won't be able to tell the difference between store-bought and homemade.

MULTICOLOURED MERINGUE KISSES

4 large egg whites, chilled

¼ teaspoon cream of tartar

1 cup (220 g) caster (superfine) sugar

½ teaspoon vanilla bean paste

medium–large piping bag fitted with a 1 cm (½ inch) round or star nozzle

small food-safe paint brush

gel paste food colouring in 2 colours

1 Preheat the oven to 100°C (200°F) fan-forced and line a baking tray with baking paper.

2 Using a hand-held mixer or a stand mixer fitted with the whisk attachment, whisk the egg whites and cream of tartar on medium speed for around 2 minutes, or until foamy and just beginning to turn white. While continuing to whisk, add the sugar very slowly (about 1 teaspoon at a time).

3 When all the sugar has been added, turn the mixer up to high speed and whisk for around 5 minutes, or until the meringue is glossy and very stiff. Mix in the vanilla on high for around 10 seconds.

4 Put the piping bag and tip together. Use a food-safe paint brush to apply long vertical stripes of food colouring gel around the inside of the piping bag. Fill the piping bag with the meringue mixture, then hold the piping bag vertically over the baking tray, almost touching the tray. Squeeze out a small amount of meringue to form the base, then gently and swiftly lift the piping bag upwards so that a nice tip is formed. Pipe the kisses onto the baking tray leaving a 1 cm (½ inch) gap between each.

5 Bake the meringues in the oven for 2–2½ hours, or until light and crisp (do not brown). Turn the oven off and leave the meringues in the oven with the door ajar to cool to room temperature.

TIP When making meringues, make sure that both the mixing bowl and whisk are clean and dry, as any moisture or fat will stop the egg whites from forming a meringue. It is also important to add the sugar slowly or the meringue will collapse.

FILLING

200 g (7 oz) cream cheese

50 g (3¾ oz) unsalted butter

1 teaspoon vanilla bean paste

1 cup (125 g) icing (confectioners') sugar

2 teaspoons lemon juice

1 Bring the cream cheese and butter to room temperature.

2 Using a hand-held mixer or a stand mixer fitted with the paddle attachment, beat the cream cheese, butter and vanilla on low speed until combined, then increase the speed to medium–high and beat for 2 minutes, or until light and fluffy.

3 Stop the mixer and add the icing sugar and lemon juice. Mix on low speed to combine. Once all of the sugar is mixed in, increase to medium–high and beat for 1 minute more, or until light and fluffy.

ASSEMBLY & DECORATION

⅓ cup (100 g) lemon curd (see p. 226, but store-bought is fine)

30 mini tart shells (found in most supermarkets, specialty grocers and online)

I To assemble the tartlets, either pipe or dollop a small amount of lemon curd into the bottom of each tart shell. Use the same method to fill with the cream cheese filling. Gently top each tart with a meringue kiss.

TIP Instead of lemon curd, you could pipe in some dulce de leche (see p. 229 or use store-bought), Biscoff spread or raspberry jam.

FOR THE FUR BABIES

THIS MAKES 2-3 MEALS FOR MY DOG PLUTO – SHE'S 10 KG (22 LB) AND HIGHLY ACTIVE. ADJUST THE SERVING SIZE ACCORDING TO YOUR DOGGIE.

Imagine the sheer joy of presenting your doggie best friend with a fancily decorated four-layer birthday cake frosted with fluffy 'buttercream'! Except this cake is made with only wholesome pooch-friendly ingredients. Pluto's favourite food in the whole wide world is chicken, so I use chicken mince to make the layers in her birthday cakes (she's had six so far), but you can use any dog-friendly protein. I like to top this cake with a show-stopping dog treat, because first impressions count! Just because it's a dog cake doesn't mean our visual standards have to slip. Our fur babies deserve only the very best.

Remember, you are the health advocate for your dog. If your dog has food allergies or other health complications, ask your vet before introducing new snacks to their diet.

DOGGIE 'CAKE'

500 g (1 lb 2 oz) chicken mince (you can use any mince though)

400 g (14 oz) mashed potato (I use frozen to save time but of course you can make it fresh)

natural food colouring, or you can use a splash of beetroot juice

a splash of milk (to thin out the mashed potato if needed)

1. Divide the mince into four portions and shape each portion into a meat patty 10 cm (4 inches) wide.

2. In a large frying pan lightly greased with cooking oil, cook the patties over medium heat for 2–3 minutes on each side, or until cooked through.

3. Allow the patties to cool and then trim the edges if needed to create a more circular shape. Make sure to give your furry little bestie any offcuts!

4. Tint the mashed potato with colouring to achieve the shade you want. If you need a slightly softer, more spreadable consistency, mix through a small amount of milk.

ASSEMBLY & DECORATION

decorative dog treats (you can use any of your dog's favourite treats; I used dog-friendly donut biscuits, found in most supermarkets and pet food stores)

1. To assemble, place one meat patty onto a small plate or cake board. Use a small spatula or butter knife to spread a 1 cm (½ inch) layer of mashed potato 'frosting' on top. Repeat the process with the remaining layers and place in the refrigerator for 15 minutes to firm up.

2. With the remaining frosting, you may choose to cover the outside using a rustic finish, or you can use a cake scraper to achieve a smooth effect on the top and side.

3. Decorate with doggie treats and serve.

STORAGE

This 'cake' can be covered and stored in the refrigerator for up to 3 days.

SUPER STRIPED PARTY CAKE

SERVES 24

Take your frosting skills to another level with this six-layered party cake. Rainbow lines of candy-striped buttercream are a surprisingly easy and super striking way to decorate a cake. No fancy cake decorating combs needed, just some standard piping bags and your trusty cake scraper. I use my ginger sponge cake recipe paired with lemon Swiss meringue buttercream for this creation – I love to use light and fluffy cake components when stacking a taller cake (to lessen the cruel impacts of gravity and avoid any lopsidedness).

. . . .

GINGER SPONGE CAKE

240 g (8 oz) unsalted butter,
   at room temperature

1½ cups (330 g) caster
   (superfine) sugar

2⅓ cups (350 g) self-raising cake
   flour or self-raising flour, sifted

1 teaspoon vanilla bean paste

6 large eggs, lightly whisked,
   at room temperature

2 teaspoons ground ginger

3 tablespoons hot water

1 Preheat the oven to 160°C (315°F) fan-forced. Grease two 15 cm (6 inch) round cake tins, at least 4 cm (1½ inches) deep, and line the bases and sides with baking paper. Ensure the baking paper creates a collar around 2.5 cm (1 inch) higher than the cake tin to allow the cake to rise. (Alternatively, you could use six 15 cm (6 inch) round single layer cake tins if you have them.)

2 Using a hand-held mixer or a stand mixer fitted with the paddle attachment, beat the butter and sugar on medium speed for 3 minutes, or until light and fluffy. Add 2 tablespoons of the flour and the vanilla, then gradually add the eggs, beating well after each addition.

3 Gently fold in the remaining flour, the ground ginger and the water.

4 Divide the batter evenly between the cake tins.

5 Bake for 30 minutes if using the two deeper cake tins, or 15–20 minutes if using the single layer cake tins, or until the centre of each cake springs back when lightly pressed. Remove from the oven and allow to cool for 10 minutes, before turning out onto a baking rack to cool completely.

6 If using the two deeper cake tins, use a cake leveller or a long, thin knife to carefully divide the cakes into three even layers. Cover and set aside until needed.

LEMON SWISS MERINGUE BUTTERCREAM

1 quantity Perfect Swiss Meringue Buttercream (see p. 233)

½ cup (175 g) lemon curd (see p. 226, or store-bought is fine)

gel paste food colouring of your choice (I used green, blue and violet)

3 medium–large piping bags fitted with a 1 cm (½ inch) round nozzle

1. Divide the Perfect Swiss Meringue Buttercream into four bowls.

2. Flavour one bowl with lemon curd and mix until combined.

3. Colour the remaining three bowls of buttercream using green, blue and violet gel colours. Place the coloured buttercreams in the piping bags.

ASSEMBLY & DECORATION

1 cup (125 g) fresh raspberries, cut in half

STORAGE

This cake is best served at room temperature. Store in an airtight container in the fridge for up to 5 days, or in the freezer for up to 1 month. Simply thaw it overnight in the fridge then bring it to room temperature before serving.

1. Working on a cake turntable, secure the bottom layer of cake onto a cake board with a small dollop of lemon buttercream and then gently twist in place. Use an offset spatula to spread a 1 cm (½ inch) layer right to the edge of the cake. Gently press eight raspberry halves, cut side down, into the buttercream. Repeat with the remaining five cake layers, lemon buttercream and raspberries, leaving the final top layer uncovered.

2. Use an offset spatula to gently crumb-coat the cake (see p. 222) with a thin layer of the remaining lemon buttercream. Chill the cake in the fridge for 10–20 minutes; this will make it much easier to pipe and smooth the buttercream stripes onto the outside.

3. Pipe a strip of the violet buttercream along the bottom edge of the cake. Working upwards, continue this process, alternating between the violet, blue and green buttercream.

4. Decorate the top by piping alternating circles of blue, green and violet buttercream, working from the outside edge inwards.

5. Take the cake scraper and place it vertically against the cake at the base. Slowly turn the cake turntable to smooth the edge and blend the lines of buttercream together.

6. Continue this process, filling any gaps with extra buttercream, until a smooth, striped effect is achieved. Use an offset spatula to smooth the top of the cake.

Secure the bottom layer of cake onto a cake board and cover with buttercream and raspberry halves. Repeat with the remaining cake layers and filling, leaving the top layer uncovered.

Use a cake scraper and an offset spatula to crumb-coat the cake, then chill the cake in the fridge.

Pipe a strip of the violet buttercream along the bottom edge of the cake. Working upwards, continue this process, alternating between the violet, blue and green buttercream.

Decorate the top by piping alternating circles of blue, green and violet buttercream, working from the outside edge inwards.

Take the cake scraper and place it vertically against the cake at the base. Slowly turn the cake turntable to smooth the edge and blend the lines of buttercream together.

Use an offset spatula to smooth the top of the cake.

SUNSHINE ON A PLATE

SERVES 16

Here's an elegant and relatively simple cake design that looks as delightful as its zesty citrus flavours taste. I made some simple fondant sugar flowers using a fondant flower cutter to decorate this cake, but you could also create delicate edible wafer paper flowers using a craft knife, scissors or craft punch to cut out the desired shapes. This cake is perfect for a picnic or an intimate garden party with friends and loved ones.

FONDANT SUGAR FLOWERS

cornflour (cornstarch), to dust

100 g (3½ oz) white fondant

100 g (3½ oz) peach fondant (you can colour white fondant using 2 drops peach food colouring)

flower-shaped fondant cutters in various sizes (available from cake decorating stores and online)

food-grade silicone or polycarbonate semisphere mould, to shape the flowers while drying (available from cake decorating stores or online; optional)

small piping bag fitted with a 3 mm (⅛ inch) circular piping tip

50 g (1¾ oz) white chocolate, melted and coloured with yellow food colouring oil or powder

1 Lightly dust a clean surface with cornflour and use a rolling pin to roll out the white and peach fondant to 2 mm (1⁄16 inch) thick. *See p. 109 for step-by-step photographs.*

2 Use floral fondant cutters to punch out flower shapes in various sizes.

3 Gently place the fondant flowers into the semisphere moulds, if using, and allow to dry for around 1 hour.

4 Meanwhile, place the melted yellow chocolate into a small piping bag and pipe a dot into the centre of each flower.

LEMON BLUEBERRY BUTTERMILK CAKE

235 g (9 oz) unsalted butter,
   at room temperature

1½ cups (300 g) white
   (granulated) sugar

1 tablespoon vanilla bean paste

4 large eggs, at room temperature

2 cups (300 g) self-raising cake
   flour or self-raising flour, sifted,
   plus 1 tablespoon extra

½ teaspoon sea salt

1 cup (250 ml) buttermilk,
   at room temperature

finely grated zest and
   juice of 2 lemons

1½ cups blueberries, fresh (260 g)
   or frozen (275 g: do not thaw)

1   Preheat the oven to 160°C (315°F) fan-forced. Grease two 18 cm (7 inch) round cake tins, at least 5 cm (2 inches) deep, and line the bases with baking paper.

2   Using a hand-held mixer or a stand mixer fitted with the paddle attachment, beat the butter on high speed until creamy. Add the sugar and beat on medium–high until light and creamy. Add the vanilla and eggs, one at a time, beating after each addition. Beat on medium until the mixture is completely combined, scraping the side and bottom of the bowl as needed.

3   Slowly add the sifted flour and salt. Beat on low speed for 5 seconds, then add the buttermilk, lemon zest and lemon juice. Lightly stir with a wooden spoon until everything is just combined.

4   Toss the blueberries with the extra 1 tablespoon of flour and fold into the batter (the batter will be extremely thick). Don't over-mix, as this can produce a tough, densely textured crumb.

5   Divide the batter evenly between the cake tins. Bake for 35–45 minutes, or until a wooden skewer inserted into the centre comes out clean. Remove from the oven and allow to cool in the tins completely before turning out onto a baking rack.

CREAM CHEESE FROSTING

750 g (1 lb 10 oz) cream cheese,
   at room temperature

80 g (2¾ oz) unsalted butter,
   at room temperature

1⅔ cups (210 g) icing
   (confectioners') sugar

2 tablespoons lemon juice

½ teaspoon vanilla bean paste

1   Using a hand-held mixer or a stand mixer fitted with the paddle attachment, beat the cream cheese and butter on high speed until fluffy. Gradually add the icing sugar while beating on low. Stop the mixer and add the lemon juice and vanilla bean paste, then beat on high until fluffy.

ASSEMBLY & DECORATION

1. Working on a cake turntable, secure the bottom layer of cake onto a cake board with a small dollop of cream cheese frosting and then gently twist in place. Use an offset spatula to spread a 1 cm (½ inch) layer of frosting right to the edge of the cake.

2. Place the second cake layer on top.

3. Use an offset spatula to gently crumb-coat the cake (see p. 222) with a thin layer of frosting. Carefully smooth the side of the cake until the desired finish is reached. Chill the cake in the refrigerator for 10–20 minutes; this will make it much easier to pipe and smooth the final layer of frosting.

4. Apply another, thicker layer of frosting to the cake and use an offset spatula to create your desired finish.

5. Decorate the cake with an adornment of fondant sugar flowers.

Lightly dust a surface with cornflour and use a rolling pin to roll out white and peach fondant to around 2 mm (1/16 inch) thick.

Use floral fondant cutters to punch out flowers of various sizes.

Gently place the fondant flowers into the semisphere moulds and allow to dry for 1 hour so that they take on a nice curved shape.

Meanwhile, place tinted melted chocolate into a small piping bag and pipe a dot into the centre of each flower.

RIPPIN' RASPBERRY SLICE

SERVES 24

I call this my Rippin' Raspberry Slice because it's a totally tastebud-tantalising combination of flavours and textures. The nostalgic combination of squidgy marshmallow, tart and tangy raspberries, smooth dark chocolate and buttery biscuit will bake the day of adults and kids alike. The crumbly biscuit base is a hero in its own right! You can easily replace the puréed raspberries in this recipe with other fruits such as passionfruit or fruit compote, or swirl through dessert spreads like dulce de leche, lemon curd, Nutella or Biscoff spread.

BASE

1 cup (150 g) self-raising flour, sifted

½ cup (110 g) caster (superfine) sugar

½ cup (35 g) shredded coconut

125 g (4½ oz) unsalted butter, melted

pinch sea salt

1   Preheat the oven to 160°C (315°F) fan-forced. Grease an 18 x 28 cm (7 x 11¼ inch) slice tin, at least 6 cm (2½ inches) deep, and line with baking paper.

2   Combine all the base ingredients in a bowl and mix well. Press into the prepared slice tin. Bake for 20 minutes, or until light golden. Remove from the oven and allow to cool in the tin on a baking rack.

MARSHMALLOW FILLING

1 cup (220 g) caster (superfine) sugar

⅓ cup (80 ml) warm water

2 tablespoons (25 g) gelatine powder

2 large egg whites, chilled

1 teaspoon vanilla bean paste

pink gel paste food colouring (optional)

1 cup (125 g) frozen raspberries, thawed and puréed

1   Place the sugar and ½ cup (125 ml) water in a large, heavy-based saucepan. Put a candy thermometer in and turn on the heat. Without stirring, allow the sugar syrup to heat and boil until it reaches 120°C (235°F) on the candy thermometer, then remove from the heat.

2   Meanwhile, place the warm water in a cup or bowl and add the gelatine powder, stirring to combine. Using a stand mixer fitted with the whisk attachment, whisk the egg whites to firm peaks.

3   Remove the sugar syrup from the heat at 120°C (235°F). Gently stir in the gelatine mixture until well combined.

4   With the stand mixer on the highest speed, carefully pour the hot sugar syrup mixture into the egg whites. Add the vanilla, food colouring (if using) and purée. Continue to whisk for 5–10 minutes, or until the mixture thickens and increases in volume. It should appear pillowy while also remaining pourable. Working quickly, pour the marshmallow over the cooked base. Cover the tin and place in the refrigerator for at least 1 hour, or until completely set.

TOPPING

200 g (7 oz) good quality dark chocolate (80% cocoa), chopped

1¼ tablespoons coconut oil

1 Put the dark chocolate and coconut oil in a clean, dry, heatproof bowl over a saucepan of just-simmering water (the water should not touch the base of the bowl). Gently stir with a silicone spatula until melted. Allow to cool slightly before spreading on top of the set marshmallow (you don't want to melt the filling). Refrigerate to set again, around 15 minutes. Bring to room temperature before cutting into bars using a knife dipped in hot water.

TIP Melting chocolate in the microwave can be a great time saver. Place the chocolate and coconut oil in a clean, dry, microwave-safe bowl and microwave at 50% power, stirring at 30-second intervals with a silicone spatula until melted.

CHOC-CARAMEL PAVLOVA CLOUD

SERVES 10-12

This chocolate pavlova with salted caramel cream and toasted macadamia nuts is the perfect way to impress your guests (and it's gluten-free too!). A dark chocolate and salted caramel drizzle give a wintry feel to this indulgent dessert. Pavlova is usually thought of as a summer treat but we all know it's a lot more fun to bend the rules!

CHOCOLATE MERINGUE

8 large egg whites (pasteurised egg whites are available in cartons at most major supermarkets), chilled

2 cups (440 g) caster (superfine) sugar

1½ tablespoons cornflour (cornstarch), sifted

2 teaspoons white vinegar

1 teaspoon vanilla bean paste

⅓ cup (40 g) Dutch cocoa, sifted

1   Preheat the oven to 120°C (235°F) fan-forced and line two baking trays with baking paper.

2   Using a hand-held mixer or stand mixer fitted with the whisk attachment, whisk the egg whites on high. When the whites have thickened, turn the mixer off and sprinkle in the caster sugar a little at a time.

3   Whisk on high speed until the whisk leaves a trail in the meringue as it goes around.

4   Turn the machine down to low only momentarily in order to add the cornflour, then return to full speed and add the white vinegar and vanilla.

5   Once the meringue has reached stiff peaks, fold the cocoa through the meringue very briefly — you want to create a swirled effect by being careful not to incorporate the cocoa completely.

6   Dollop the meringue mixture onto the trays to form three discs 15 cm (6 inches) in diameter. You may need an offset spatula to help you gently spread the meringue outwards.

7   Place both baking trays into the oven and immediately reduce the oven to 100°C (200°F) fan-forced. Bake for 2 hours. Once baked, turn the oven off and allow the meringue to cool completely in the oven.

TIP   Make sure that both the mixing bowl and the whisk are clean and dry, as any moisture or fat will stop the egg whites from forming a meringue. It is also important to add the sugar slowly or the meringue will collapse.

ASSEMBLY & DECORATION

2 cups (500 ml) thick (double) cream

1½ cups (230 g) macadamia nuts, halved or chopped, toasted

200 g (7 oz) salted caramel (see p. 228, but store-bought is fine too), plus extra for drizzling

50 g (1¾ oz) dark chocolate, melted, for drizzling

(see p. 228, but store-bought is fine too)

STORAGE

This pavlova is best enjoyed on the same day as assembly. It can be stored in an airtight container in the refrigerator for up to 3 days.

You can make the meringues 1 week ahead of time and store them in an airtight container in a dry environment until needed for assembly.

1 Using a hand-held mixer or stand mixer fitted with the whisk attachment, whip the cream until stiff peaks form.

2 Place a chocolate meringue disc on a serving plate. Dollop whipped cream into the centre of the chocolate meringue and push to the outer edge. Scatter some toasted macadamia nuts on top and drizzle with salted caramel. Repeat this process twice more until you have three layers.

3 Use a spoon to drizzle melted chocolate over the top of the pavlova. Add a final drizzle of salted caramel and a sprinkling of macadamias before serving.

WARM CARAMEL-APPLE HUG

SERVES 12

In my humble opinion, this cake ticks so many dessert boxes and offers multiple warm hugs from the inside out. After the impressive inverting (do this in front of the guests if you're feeling fancy), the topping's caramel juices seep down into the cake and add unbeatable flavour and moisture. What you may love most – besides the flavours, of course – is that there's no fancy decoration required. The eye-catching pattern on top is literally baked into the cake! It's best served warm.

CARAMEL

1 cup (220 g) caster (superfine) sugar

25 g (1 oz) unsalted butter

pinch sea salt

1   Preheat the oven to 170°C (325°F) fan-forced. Grease a 24 cm (9½ inch) round cake tin, at least 6 cm (2½ inches) deep, and line the base and side with baking paper.

2   Combine the caster sugar and 2 tablespoons water in a small saucepan and use a wooden spoon to stir over low heat until the sugar dissolves. Increase the heat to medium and cook, without stirring, until the mixture transforms into golden caramel (this should take around 10 minutes). Add the butter and salt and stir until combined. Pour the caramel into the cake tin and set aside.

APPLE CAKE

3 granny smith apples

1 tablespoon lemon juice

175 g (6 oz) unsalted butter, at room temperature

½ cup (100 g) lightly packed soft brown sugar

200 g (7 oz) dulce de leche (or any store-bought type of caramel spread is just fine. Try Biscoff if you can find it!)

1 teaspoon vanilla bean paste

2 large eggs, at room temperature

1¼ cups (185 g) self-raising cake flour or self-raising flour, sifted

1 cup (100 g) almond meal

pouring caramel (store-bought or homemade), to serve (optional)

vanilla bean yoghurt, ice cream, crème fraîche, or whipped cream, to serve

1   Peel, core and slice the apples into circles 5 mm–1 cm (¼–½ inch) thick, placing them in a bowl with the lemon juice as you go to prevent them from browning.

2   Cover the caramel with overlapping circles of the apple.

3   Using a hand-held mixer or stand mixer fitted with the paddle attachment, beat the butter and brown sugar on medium speed for 2–3 minutes, until thick and pale, then add the dulce de leche and vanilla and beat again for 1 minute more or until fluffy. Beat in the eggs one at a time, beating well after each addition.

4   Fold in the flour and almond meal, then transfer the mixture into the cake tin. Bake for 40–45 minutes, or until a wooden skewer inserted into the centre comes out clean. Rest the cake in the tin for 10 minutes, then carefully invert it onto a plate. Drizzle the caramel from the tin on top of the cake. Add extra pouring caramel, if desired, and serve with vanilla bean yoghurt, ice cream, crème fraîche or whipped cream.

STORAGE

This cake is best served warm or at room temperature. It can be stored in an airtight container in the refrigerator for up to 5 days. Reheat before serving for leftovers.

next level

Conquer these reputation-making bakes and
you'll be the go-to cake dealer for every occasion

CHOCOLATE CHRISTMAS SURPRISE

SERVES 24–30

This whimsical cake is an irresistibly attractive centrepiece for Christmas Day celebrations. The chocolate bauble decorations are filled with surprise treats and designed to be smashed open; it's super delightful for kids (I shriek with glee too!). I like to make extra chocolate baubles to decorate the table or to give as gifts. When stored properly they can be made weeks ahead of time, which should hopefully save you some stress in the lead-up to any Christmas party prep. I use my trusty chocolate mudcake recipe here as it holds up in all weather conditions and stays moist for days, but you can also use any other sturdy cake, such as caramel mudcake or white chocolate mudcake.

CHOCOLATE MUDCAKE

melted butter or cooking oil spray, for greasing

400 g (14 oz) unsalted butter, chopped

400 g (14 oz) good quality dark chocolate, chopped

1½ cups (375 ml) hot water

1 cup (105 g) Dutch cocoa powder, sifted

⅓ cup (80 ml) instant coffee

2 teaspoons vanilla extract

2 cups (440 g) caster (superfine) sugar

6 large eggs, at room temperature

1½ cups (220 g) self-raising flour, sifted

1 Preheat the oven to 160°C (315°F) fan-forced. Grease five 18 cm (7 inch) single layer round cake tins and line the base of each with baking paper.

2 Combine the butter, dark chocolate, hot water, cocoa, coffee and vanilla in a medium saucepan. Heat over low heat, whisking constantly, until smooth and well combined. Remove from the heat and set aside until the mixture is lukewarm.

3 Using a hand-held mixer or a stand mixer fitted with the whisk attachment, whisk the sugar and eggs on high speed for 2 minutes, or until pale and creamy. Whisk in the chocolate mixture until well combined. Add the flour and whisk again.

4 Divide the mixture equally between the cake tins and bake for 20–25 minutes (rotating the tins halfway through baking if needed), or until a wooden skewer inserted into the centre of each cake comes out almost clean. (The centre of your mudcakes will still be quite sticky, almost gooey, but will come together once cooled.)

5 Remove the cakes from the oven and allow to cool completely in the tins. Once cooled, remove the cakes from the tins, cover and set aside until it's time to assemble the cake.

CHOCOLATE BAUBLES

800 g (1 lb 12 oz) white chocolate melts (compound works perfectly but couverture tastes best)

chocolate colouring powder or oil, in assorted colours (I used pink and green; you could also replace the same amount of white chocolate with two different colours of Candy Melts)

small food-safe paint brush

3 food-grade silicone or polycarbonate semisphere moulds; mine were 2.5 cm/1 inch, 5 cm/2 inches and 7.5 cm/3 inches in diameter (available from cake decorating stores or online)

100 g (3½ oz) white fondant

½ teaspoon Tylose powder (available from cake decorating stores)

wooden skewer (to help assemble your 'bauble hanger')

edible gold paint or edible gold lustre mixed into a paste using cake decorator's rose spirit (available from cake decorating stores) or vodka

2 cups (360 g) M&M's or other small candies of your choice

1   Put the chocolate in a clean, dry, heatproof bowl over a saucepan of just-simmering water (the water should not touch the base of the bowl). Gently stir with a silicone spatula until melted. (If using couverture chocolate, temper the chocolate as per the manufacturer's instructions.)

2   Place 4 tablespoons of the melted white chocolate in a small bowl, and another 4 tablespoons in another small bowl. Colour these as desired (I used pink and green). Use a food-safe paint brush to create decorative strokes with the coloured chocolate on the inside of each cavity of the moulds (you can use the photos as a guide), then leave to set.

3   Fill the moulds completely with the remaining melted chocolate. Firmly tap the mould on your bench to release any air bubbles. Use the cake scraper to scrape across the top of the mould to remove any excess chocolate. Allow the chocolate to thicken slightly (around 5–10 minutes).

4   Lay a sheet of baking paper on the bench then turn the mould upside-down and let the chocolate mix run back out onto the baking paper. Tap the side of the mould to assist the process.

5   Once the chocolate has finished dripping out, scrape again before turning the mould back up the right way. You should have a nice, smooth layer of chocolate in your moulds. (The excess chocolate on the baking paper can be re-used at another date but should be kept airtight and at room temperature until required.) Turn the mould back upside-down and place it face down with some force on a tray lined with baking paper to encourage the chocolate to pool downwards — this will create a thicker rim around the inner edge of the semispheres. Set the semispheres by placing the moulds in the refrigerator for 30 minutes or the freezer for 15 minutes or leave at room temperature overnight.

6   Mix the fondant with the Tylose powder. Model the fondant with your fingers and the wooden skewer to form at least five hanging tips for your baubles. Put aside to dry completely, around 20 minutes, then decorate with edible gold paint or lustre.

7   Once the spheres have set, gently remove them from the moulds. Place both halves of each sphere on a warm frying pan or warm oven tray for 1 second only — any longer and your spheres will melt too far and lose their shape! Fill one half with candies and then carefully press both halves together and hold until completely set. Repeat this process with the remaining halves.

8   Decorate your chocolate baubles with splashes of edible gold paint. Once dry, adhere the hanging tips of your baubles to the finished chocolate spheres with a small amount of melted chocolate.

TIP   To melt chocolate in the microwave, place the chocolate in a clean, dry, microwave-safe bowl and microwave at 50% power, stirring at 30-second intervals with a silicone spatula until melted.

Use a food-safe brush to paint decorative strokes of coloured melted chocolate on the inside of each cavity and allow to set. Once dry, fill the moulds completely with white chocolate.

Scrape the mould to remove excess chocolate, then turn it upside-down on a sheet of baking paper to let the chocolate run out. When the chocolate has finished dripping out, scrape again. You should have a smooth layer of chocolate in your moulds.

Make at least five fondant hanging tips for your baubles. Once dry, decorate with edible gold paint or lustre.

Place both halves of each sphere on a warm frying pan or warm oven tray for 1 second only — any longer and your spheres will melt too far!

Fill one half of each sphere with candies and then carefully press both halves together and hold until completely set. Repeat this process with the remaining halves.

Decorate the chocolate baubles with splashes of edible gold paint. Once dry, stick the hanging tips onto the baubles with a small amount of melted chocolate.

WATERCOLOURED SWISS MERINGUE BUTTERCREAM

1 quantity Perfect Swiss Meringue
  Buttercream (see p. 233)

different gel paste food colours
  of your choice (I used
  red and pink colours)

1 Place three-quarters of the Perfect Swiss Meringue Buttercream mixture in a separate bowl and set aside at room temperature in a cool environment until needed.

2 Divide the remaining buttercream evenly between two bowls and colour each portion with your choice of gel paste food colour.

3 Cover the bowls with plastic wrap and set aside.

ASSEMBLY & DECORATION

large cake scraper (I used a
  30 cm/12 inch cake scraper)

small food-safe paint brush

edible gold paint or edible gold
  lustre mixed into a paste using
  cake decorator's rose spirit
  (available from cake decorating
  stores) or vodka (optional)

1 Working on a cake turntable, secure the bottom layer of cake onto a cake board with a small dollop of the white Swiss meringue buttercream and then gently press in place. Use an offset spatula to spread a 5 mm (¼ inch) layer of white Swiss meringue buttercream right to the edge of the cake.

2 Repeat this process until you have used all the cake layers, leaving the final top layer uncovered. Use an offset spatula to gently crumb-coat the cake (see p. 222) with a thin layer of white Swiss meringue buttercream and set aside in the refrigerator for 10–20 minutes, or until firm.

3 Apply generous amounts of the two different coloured Swiss meringue buttercreams all over the outside of your cake. Now, using a cake scraper, carefully blend and smooth the side and top of your cake to achieve a watercolour look. Place your cake in the refrigerator for at least 30 minutes to firm and cool.

4 Make the white chocolate ganache (see opposite page) then, using a metal spoon, apply the ganache drips to your cake one drip at a time, working 5 cm (2 inches) from the edge of the cake and gently working the ganache over the side. If your ganache is too thick, simply heat it in the microwave for 10 seconds. Fill the top of your cake with ganache until completely covered. To prevent the ganache drips from cascading any further, place the cake in the refrigerator again for at least 30 minutes.

5 Adorn the cake with an arrangement of your chocolate baubles. Finally, using a food-safe paint brush, flick gold paint decoratively over the cake (if desired). Set your finished cake aside in a cool environment until you're ready to serve it.

EASY WHITE CHOCOLATE GANACHE

500 g (1 lb 2 oz) white chocolate melts

1 cup (250 ml) single (pure) cream

2 drops whitening gel paste colour (optional)

1 Place the white chocolate in a heatproof bowl. In a separate heatproof bowl, microwave the cream for 30–40 seconds or until it just starts to boil.

2 Pour the hot cream over the white chocolate, making sure that most of the white chocolate is covered. Let it sit for 5 minutes, then stir gently until the white chocolate has melted completely and the mixture is smooth. If needed, microwave for another 10 seconds at a time, stirring gently at intervals, until smooth. Colour with the whitening gel until the desired colour is achieved.

3 Set aside until the ganache cools and thickens. It should be thick enough so that it falls in a slow stream from a spoon. If needed, chill it in the refrigerator briefly, about 5–10 minutes, and then stir again until smooth.

SUCH A TART

SERVES 12-16

I whip up this epic tart whenever I really want to impress – the colours of the ganache, marshmallows and passionfruit contrast just beautifully, making this decadent dessert a feast for the eyes. The buttery biscuit crust, smooth coffee ganache and fluffy raspberry marshmallows can all be prepared in advance, so with some basic planning this recipe is much easier than it looks!

BISCUIT CRUST

400 g (14 oz) of your favourite semi-sweet biscuits (I used half Shredded Wheatmeal biscuits and half Butternut Snap biscuits)

100 g (3½ oz) unsalted butter, melted

1 Grease a 23 cm (9 inch) tart tin with a removable base, 6 cm (2½ inches) deep, and line with baking paper (or for mini tarts use 12 x 10 cm/4 inch loose-bottomed tart tins). Place the biscuits in a food processor and process until fine crumbs form. Add the melted butter and pulse until well combined (the mixture should clump together when squeezed with your fingers).

2 Place the mixture into the tart tin (or divide among smaller tart tins). Use the back of a large metal spoon to evenly press the mix into the bottom and up the side of the tin. Place the tart tin in the refrigerator to chill for at least 30 minutes.

COFFEE LIQUEUR GANACHE

500 g (1 lb 2 oz) good quality dark chocolate

1¼ cups (310 ml) thick (double) cream

½ cup (125 ml) coffee liqueur (I used Mr Black Spirits) or for a non-alcoholic ganache, use ½ cup/125 ml espresso. And if you're not a coffee fan, just add an extra ½ cup/125 ml thick (double) cream

1 Place the chocolate in a large, heatproof bowl. Heat the cream in a small saucepan over low heat, stirring often. Once the cream starts to bubble, remove it from the heat.

2 Carefully pour the hot cream over the chocolate and leave it to sit for 2 minutes. Stir well with a whisk (or you can emulsify with a stick blender if you have one) and scrape down the sides of the bowl with a spatula until the mixture is glossy. Add the coffee liqueur and whisk until combined. Leave to thicken in the refrigerator for approximately 30 minutes – it should be still pourable but not hot.

RASPBERRY MARSHMALLOWS

1 cup (220 g) caster
   (superfine) sugar

½ cup (125 ml) warm water

2 tablespoons (25 g)
   gelatine powder

2 large egg whites, chilled

1 teaspoon vanilla bean paste

⅓ cup (90 g) puréed
   raspberries (I use frozen)

pink gel paste food
   colouring (optional)

1 cup (90 g) desiccated coconut

1   Grease a 23 cm (9 inch) square cake tin, at least 6 cm (2½ inches) deep, and line with baking paper.

2   Place the sugar and ½ cup (125 ml) water in a large, heavy-based saucepan. Put a candy thermometer in and turn on the heat. Without stirring, allow the sugar syrup to heat and boil until it reaches 120°C (235°F) on the candy thermometer.

3   Meanwhile, place the warm water in a cup or bowl and add the gelatine powder, stirring to combine. Using a stand mixer fitted with the whisk attachment, whisk the egg whites to firm peaks.

4   Remove the sugar syrup from the heat at 120°C (235°F). Gently stir in the gelatine mixture until well combined.

5   With the stand mixer on the highest speed, carefully pour the hot sugar syrup mixture into the egg whites. Add the vanilla, raspberries and colouring (if using). Continue to whisk for 5–10 minutes, or until the mixture thickens and increases in volume. It should appear pillowy while also remaining pourable.

6   Working quickly, pour the marshmallow into the tin and firmly tap it on your bench until level. Use a spatula if needed to push the marshmallow into the corners of the tin. Cover and place into the refrigerator for at least 1 hour, or until completely set.

7   To remove the marshmallow from the tin, cover your hands in cooking oil spray to prevent the marshmallow from sticking and gently lift up the sides of the baking paper. Place the marshmallow onto a greased chopping board. Grease a long, sharp knife and slice the marshmallows into cubes. Place the desiccated coconut in a bowl and roll each marshmallow generously in coconut to coat.

ASSEMBLY & DECORATION

1¼ cups (310 ml) thick
   (double) cream, whipped

½ cup (125 ml) passionfruit pulp
   (the canned version is fine too)

1 cup (125 g) fresh raspberries

1   Pour the coffee liqueur ganache into the tart (or smaller tarts) and smooth to level. Refrigerate for at least 1 hour or until set.

2   Once the ganache has firmed, dollop whipped cream on top of the ganache. Now it's time to adorn your tart with a nice drizzling of passionfruit, some fluffy raspberry marshmallows and a studding of fresh raspberries. Enjoy chilled or at room temperature.

STORAGE

The tart will keep in an airtight container in the refrigerator for up to 5 days. Store any left-over marshmallows in an airtight container in the refrigerator for up to 7 days.

GREEN-THUMB EDIBLE TERRARIUMS

SERVES 8

Making mini edible terrariums is a really fun way to nurture your inner green thumb while creating some dessert magic. These super cute centrepieces are 100% edible and made with luscious chocolate mousse, crumbled cookies and pretty fondant succulents. I first created an edible terrarium as a collaboration with my green-thumbed Hairy Godmother and best friend Jane (who runs A Loft Story hairdressing salon in Sydney). As a duo, we held terrarium workshops for our inner-city community, surrounded by the beauty of her tranquil and lush jungle studio.

CHOCOLATE MOUSSE

200 g (7 oz) good quality dark chocolate

50 g (1¾ oz) unsalted butter

4 large eggs, separated, at room temperature

2 tablespoons caster (superfine) sugar

1 cup (250 ml) thick (double) cream, whipped

1 Put the dark chocolate and butter in a clean, dry, heatproof bowl over a saucepan of just-simmering water (the water should not touch the base of the bowl). Gently stir with a silicone spatula until melted. Set aside.

2 Using a hand-held mixer or a stand mixer fitted with the whisk attachment, whisk the egg whites until soft peaks form. Sprinkle the caster sugar on top and whisk again until the mixture is thick and the sugar has dissolved.

3 Stir the egg yolks into the cooled chocolate mixture.

4 Fold the chocolate mixture and cream into the whisked egg whites.

5 Spoon into a large bowl and refrigerate for at least 3 hours.

TIP Melting chocolate in the microwave can be a great time saver. Place the chocolate and butter in a clean, dry, microwave-safe bowl and microwave at 50% power, stirring at 30-second intervals with a silicone spatula until melted.

FONDANT SUCCULENTS

150 g (5½ oz) white fondant

cornflour (cornstarch), for dusting

gel paste food colouring
(I used pink, orange,
green and purple)

1 Divide the fondant into as many colours as you'd like to make. I recommend wearing disposable gloves while colouring fondant, to avoid staining your hands. Dust your work surface with cornflour and flatten out one portion of fondant into a disc. Place a few drops of food colouring in the centre and fold the sides over so the colouring is in the middle of a fondant ball. Knead the fondant like bread dough, adding more colouring until you get the shade you want. Wrap the fondant in plastic wrap to prevent it from drying out and repeat with the remaining fondant and colours.

2 There is no right or wrong when it comes to shaping your colourful mini succulents but, if you're stuck for ideas, follow the instructions opposite.

ASSEMBLY & DECORATION

1 cup desiccated coconut

2 drops green food colouring liquid

8 small clear bowls or clear glasses

16 (180 g) Oreo cookies,
crushed (or you could use
loosely crumbled chocolate
cake or muffins)

¾ cup (120 g) edible chocolate
rocks (available online)

handful of edible flowers
(available from specialty
grocers and online; optional)

1 Place the coconut and green food colouring liquid into a bag or takeaway container, seal and shake until the coconut turns green to resemble grass.

2 Fill the eight small bowls or glasses, alternating between your ingredients (crushed Oreos, chocolate mousse, coconut, etc) to create the different layers of your terrariums. Lastly, add the chocolate rocks and gently rest a fondant succulent on top. Scatter with some edible flower petals (if using).

STORAGE

I recommend assembling the terrariums on the day of serving, so the layers don't get too soggy. Leftovers can be stored in the refrigerator for 3–4 days.

The mousse can be made ahead and stored in an airtight container in the fridge for 3 days before using. The fondant succulents can be made up to 1 month in advance. Allow them to dry out at room temperature before storing them in an airtight container in a cool, dark environment away from moisture.

To make succulent leaves, roll the fondant into small balls. Pinch one side of the ball then press down on the centre of the ball with a ball tool to create a leaf shape. Stack and layer the leaves as shown. Use 10 leaves for an open style mini succulent with buds (place two tiny round balls in the centre for the buds). For a fuller looking succulent use around 15 leaves. If required, use a tiny amount of water or sugar glue to stick the leaves together.

Assemble each terrarium by layering alternating ingredients (crushed Oreos, chocolate mousse, coconut, etc). Finish with a layer of colourful chocolate rocks then gently place a fondant succulent on top and scatter with edible flower petals (if using).

OOZY ICE-CREAM CAKE

SERVES 24-30

This cake was born out of three things I loved growing up: ice cream, cake and the oozy, glossy slime motif on the cover of *Goosebumps* novels. In fact, most of my 'drip cakes' are inspired by gloriously viscous goo and this design was the very first of my drip cakes. The original design has become my most well-loved party cake to date and it truly fills me with joy seeing home bakers worldwide re-create this cake for that special kiddo in their lives (big and small).

LEMON SPONGE CAKE

320 g (11¼ oz) unsalted butter, at room temperature

2 cups (440 g) caster (superfine) sugar

3 teaspoons finely grated lemon zest

3 cups (450 g) self-raising cake flour or self-raising flour, sifted

8 large eggs, lightly whisked, at room temperature

⅓ cup (80 ml) hot water

1   Preheat the oven to 160°C (315°F) fan-forced. Grease four 18 cm (7 inch) round cake tins, 4 cm (1½ inches) deep, and line the bases with baking paper (don't fret if you don't have enough cake tins — you can bake the cake batter in batches until four single layers are baked).

2   Using a hand-held mixer or a stand mixer fitted with the paddle attachment, beat the butter, sugar and lemon zest until light, pale and creamy. Briefly beat in 5 tablespoons of the flour, then gradually add the eggs one by one, beating well after each addition.

3   Gently fold in the remaining flour and the hot water. Divide the mixture equally between the prepared tins.

4   Bake for 20–25 minutes, or until the centre of each cake springs back when lightly pressed. Remove from the oven and allow to cool for 5 minutes, before turning out onto a baking rack to cool completely. Cover and set aside until needed for cake assembly.

PERFECT SWISS MERINGUE BUTTERCREAM

1 quantity Perfect Swiss Meringue Buttercream (see p. 233)

1   Make the buttercream, cover the bowl with plastic wrap and set aside at room temperature in a cool environment until needed.

WHITE CHOCOLATE GANACHE

300 g (10½ oz) white
   chocolate, chopped

1¼ cups (310 ml) single
   (pure) cream

blue oil-based food colouring
   or food colouring powder
   (I used baby blue chocolate
   colouring oil)

1. Place the white chocolate in a heatproof bowl. In a separate heatproof bowl, microwave the cream for 30–40 seconds or until it just starts to boil.

2. Pour the hot cream over the white chocolate, making sure that most of the white chocolate is covered. Let it sit for 5 minutes, then stir gently until the white chocolate has melted completely and the mixture is smooth. If needed, microwave for another 10 seconds at a time, stirring gently at intervals, until smooth. Colour until the desired shade is achieved.

3. Set aside until the ganache cools and thickens. It should be thick enough so that it falls in a slow stream from a spoon. If needed, chill it in the refrigerator briefly, about 5–10 minutes, and then stir again until smooth.

GIANT ICE-CREAM CONE CAKE POP

large plain muffin (or you can
   use left-over cake mixed with
   softened cream cheese)

300 g (10½ oz) white
   chocolate, chopped

blue oil-based food colouring
   or food colouring powder
   (I used baby blue chocolate
   colouring oil)

large waffle ice-cream cone

1. Press and squish the muffin with your hands to form it into a smooth ball. Refrigerate until firm.

2. Place the chocolate in a clean, dry, microwave-safe bowl and microwave at 50% power, stirring at 30-second intervals with a silicone spatula until melted. Add the food colouring one drop at a time until the desired shade is achieved.

3. Dip the mouth of the waffle cone into the melted chocolate, then gently shake off any excess chocolate. Allow it to set upside-down on baking paper. *See page 141 for step-by-step photographs.*

4. Re-melt the chocolate if necessary and use two spoons to roll the muffin ball or cake pop in the melted chocolate until completely covered.

5. Place the ball onto a small chopping board or plate lined with baking paper and cover with some more melted chocolate. Carefully place the cone on top, to resemble an upside-down melting ice-cream cone. Set aside in the refrigerator for 5–10 minutes, or until the chocolate has completely set.

ASSEMBLY & DECORATION

1 cup (320 g) blueberry jam

2 large piping bags fitted with 1.5–
2 cm (⅝–¾ inch) round nozzles

rainbow confetti sprinkles or
other sprinkles of your choice

1   Working on a cake turntable, secure the bottom layer of cake
onto a cake board with a small dollop of Swiss meringue
buttercream and then gently twist in place.

2   Place the Swiss meringue buttercream and the jam into two
separate piping bags. Use the Swiss meringue buttercream to
outline the edge of the cake layer and create a spiral pattern into
the centre. Fill with jam, being careful not to fill higher than the
buttercream layer. Place in the refrigerator for 10 minutes, to firm.

3   Repeat this process until you have used all the cake layers, leaving
the final top layer uncovered. Use the remaining Swiss meringue
buttercream and an offset spatula to apply a thin crumb-coat
(see p. 222) over the whole cake.

4   Apply another layer of Swiss meringue buttercream to the cake
and use a cake scraper to smooth the side (see p. 223). Finally, use
an offset spatula to smooth the top of the cake by gently pulling
inwards from the outer edge of the cake into the centre, cleaning
the excess buttercream off the spatula with each scrape. Return
to the refrigerator to chill completely.

5   Place the upside-down ice-cream cone on top of the chilled cake
and carefully spoon ganache over the top and sides of the ice-cream
'scoop' until completely covered. Spoon ganache around the top
edges of the cake, allowing it to drip over and create the effect of
melting ice cream. (You may want to test your drip technique down
the side of a chilled bowl or a silicone spatula first.)

6   For a final decorative touch, lightly toss some confetti sprinkles over
and around the sides of the melting ice-cream cone.

Dip the mouth of the waffle cone into the melted chocolate, then gently shake off any excess chocolate.

Use two spoons to roll the muffin ball or cake pop in the melted chocolate until completely covered.

Place the ball onto some baking paper and cover with more melted chocolate.

Carefully place the cone upside-down on top of the ball of 'ice cream' and allow to set.

Place the upside-down ice-cream cone on top of the chilled cake and carefully spoon ganache over the top and sides of the ice-cream 'scoop' until completely covered.

Spoon ganache around the top edges of the cake, allowing it to drip over and create the effect of melting ice cream.

MARSHMALLOW BUNNY BUTTS

SERVES 20-24

The soft and snuggly appearance of this creation honestly fills me with glee – an angelic vanilla velvet cake covered with marshmallow frosting and studded with an entire family of homemade vanilla and coconut marshmallow bunny bottoms. It's a novelty spin on my already novel Pom Pom cake and, quite possibly, the most delightful cake you'll ever lay eyes on.

VANILLA VELVET CAKE

2¾ cups (410 g) self-raising cake flour or self-raising flour

½ teaspoon bicarbonate of soda (baking soda)

½ teaspoon sea salt flakes

1¼ cups (275 g) caster (superfine) sugar

1 cup (250 ml) vegetable oil

2 teaspoons vanilla extract

3 large eggs (for the whitest cake, substitute 4 egg whites), at room temperature

1½ cups (375 ml) buttermilk, at room temperature

1 Preheat the oven to 160°C (315°F) fan-forced. Grease a 23 cm (9 inch) ovenproof glass bowl, at least 15 cm (6 inches) deep, with cooking oil spray (I use a Pyrex glass bowl).

2 Sift together the flour, bicarbonate of soda, salt and sugar. Set aside.

3 Using a hand-held mixer or stand mixer fitted with the whisk attachment, whisk together the vegetable oil and vanilla on high speed until frothed. Whisk in the eggs, one at a time.

4 Gently fold through the dry ingredients in three divisions, alternating with two divisions of the buttermilk. Mix until just combined, being careful not to over-mix.

5 Pour the mixture into the prepared glass bowl and bake for 40–45 minutes, or until a wooden skewer inserted into the centre comes out clean. Stand the cake in the bowl for 1 hour, before turning out onto a baking rack, top-side down, to cool completely.

6 Trim the bottom to level, if needed. Cover with plastic wrap or a clean, damp tea towel and set aside until assembly.

MARSHMALLOW PUFFS

3 food-grade silicone or
    polycarbonate semisphere
    moulds, greased with
    cooking oil spray; mine were
    2 cm/¾ inch, 5 cm/2 inches
    and 9 cm/3½ inches in
    diameter (available from cake
    decorating stores or online)

2¼ cups (495 g) caster
    (superfine) sugar

½ cup (125 ml) warm water

¼ cup (40 g) gelatine powder

1 teaspoon vanilla bean paste

3 large egg whites, chilled

gel paste food colouring
    of your choice (I used
    pink, teal and violet)

3 large piping bags fitted with
    2 cm (¾ inch) round nozzles

2 cups (180 g) desiccated coconut

1   Place the greased silicone moulds on a baking tray. Place the sugar and 1 cup (250 ml) water in a large, heavy-based saucepan. Put a candy thermometer in and turn on the heat. Without stirring, allow the sugar syrup to heat and boil until it reaches 120°C (235°F) on the candy thermometer.

2   Meanwhile, place the ½ cup (125 ml) warm water in a cup or bowl and add the gelatine powder, stirring to combine. Add the vanilla. Using a stand mixer fitted with the whisk attachment, whisk the egg whites to firm peaks.

3   Remove the sugar syrup from the heat at 120°C (235°F). Gently stir in the gelatine mixture until well combined.

4   With the stand mixer on the highest speed, carefully pour the hot sugar syrup into the egg whites. Continue to whisk for 5–10 minutes, or until the mixture thickens and increases in volume. It should appear pillowy while also remaining pourable. Working quickly, divide the mixture between three microwave-safe bowls, fold through the gel colours until mixed through, then place each marshmallow colour in a piping bag. If any of the marshmallow begins to set before you are able to place it into piping bags, simply gently reheat it in the microwave for 20 seconds, or until re-melted. Quickly pipe the marshmallow into all the silicone moulds, until level. Place the baking tray with the moulds into the refrigerator for at least 1 hour, or until completely set.

5   To remove the marshmallows from the moulds, lightly oil your hands with a small amount of cooking oil spray and gently pop them out one by one, rolling each one generously in the coconut.

TIP   You can also flavour your marshmallow with fruit purée or natural flavouring extracts.

BUNNY FEET & TAILS

1⅓ cups (200 g) white chocolate
    melts (or white Candy Melts),
    plus ⅔ cup (100 g) extra
    white chocolate melts and
    pink chocolate colouring (or
    ⅔ cup/100 g pink Candy Melts)

2 large piping bags fitted with
    3 mm (⅛ inch) round nozzles

1   Melt the 1⅓ cups (200 g) white chocolate and place it in a piping bag. Pipe bunny feet (see p. 147) onto a sheet of baking paper. You will need approximately 20 sets of feet (depending on the number of marshmallows you would like to decorate), but I suggest you make extra just to be safe – you can always store them for later use if you have leftovers.

2   Pipe approximately 20 round bunny tails onto baking paper (see p. 147). Save the remaining white chocolate for assembling the cake.

3   Melt the extra ⅔ cup (100 g) white chocolate with the pink colouring. Transfer it to a piping bag and pipe the pink middle section of each bunny foot as well as the bunny toes (see p. 147). Allow the feet to completely set on a sheet of baking paper (you can speed up the process by popping them into the refrigerator).

MARSHMALLOW FROSTING & ASSEMBLY

1 cup (220 g) caster (superfine) sugar

½ cup (110 g) glucose or corn syrup

4 large egg whites, chilled

¼ teaspoon cream of tartar

1 teaspoon vanilla bean paste

1   In a small saucepan, combine the sugar, glucose syrup and ¼ cup (60 ml) water.

2   Bring to a boil over medium heat and continue to cook, without stirring, until the mixture reaches 115°C (240°F) on a candy thermometer (or when a teaspoonful of the mixture dropped into iced water forms a soft ball that holds its shape when cool). Remove from the heat.

3   Meanwhile, using a stand mixer fitted with the whisk attachment, whisk the egg whites, cream of tartar and vanilla paste until soft peaks form.

4   With the stand mixer on medium–high speed, slowly pour the sugar syrup down the side of the bowl in a thin continuous stream. Continue to whisk the frosting for around 5 minutes, or until it forms stiff peaks.

5   Frost the cake immediately with the frosting while it is still slightly warm as it is easier to spread smoothly than if allowed to cool completely.

6   Once iced, decorate with the marshmallow puffs by starting at the top and working down, alternating between different sizes and colours of bunny butts.

7   Re-melt the left-over white chocolate in the piping bag and use this to attach the bunny feet and tails to the marshmallow puffs.

TIP   If you'd prefer to decorate this cake ahead of time or would like to allow for longer storage time once decorated, simply replace the marshmallow frosting with cream cheese frosting, Swiss meringue buttercream or white chocolate ganache.

Pipe white chocolate bunny feet and bunny tails onto a sheet of baking paper.

Use pink coloured white chocolate to pipe the pink middle section of each bunny foot and three bunny toes.

To decorate your iced cake, place the marshmallow bunny butts from the top to the bottom of the cake, alternating between different sizes and colours.

Use white chocolate to attach the bunny feet and tails to the marshmallow puffs.

SUPER-KAWAII NARWHAL CAKE

SERVES 16

Is it a narwhal? Is it a whale? Is it a swimming unicorn? Who knows! But it IS a dreamy vanilla velvet cake filled with Swiss meringue buttercream. I absolutely adore narwhals – they are such magical creatures that it's hard to believe they aren't mythical. While this cake is totally adorable, narwhals themselves are mightily impressive. Their tusk, which is actually a tooth, can grow up to 2.7 metres (9 feet) long and they can live up to 50 years. I first created this for my friend Jane, who loves all things super-kawaii.

VANILLA VELVET CAKE

2¾ cups (410 g) self-raising cake flour or self-raising flour

½ teaspoon bicarbonate of soda (baking soda)

½ teaspoon sea salt flakes

1¼ cups (275 g) caster (superfine) sugar

1 cup (250 ml) vegetable oil

2 teaspoons vanilla extract

3 large eggs (for the whitest cake, substitute 4 egg whites), at room temperature

1½ cups (375 ml) buttermilk, at room temperature

1 Preheat the oven to 160°C (315°F) fan-forced. Grease a 23 cm (9 inch) ovenproof glass bowl, at least 15 cm (6 inches) deep, with cooking oil spray (I use a Pyrex glass bowl).

2 Sift together the flour, bicarbonate of soda, salt and sugar. Set aside.

3 Using a hand-held mixer or stand mixer fitted with the whisk attachment, whisk together the vegetable oil and vanilla on high speed until frothed. Whisk in the eggs, one at a time.

4 Gently fold through the dry ingredients in three divisions, alternating with two divisions of the buttermilk. Mix until just combined, being careful not to over-mix.

5 Pour the mixture into the prepared glass bowl and bake for 40–45 minutes, or until a wooden skewer inserted into the centre comes out clean. Stand the cake in the bowl for 1 hour, before turning out onto a baking rack, top-side down, to cool completely.

6 Trim the bottom to level, if needed. Cover with plastic wrap or a clean, damp tea towel and set aside until assembly.

SKY BLUE SWISS MERINGUE BUTTERCREAM

1½ cups (330 g) caster (superfine) sugar

8 large egg whites (pasteurised egg whites are available in cartons at most major supermarkets), chilled

500 g (1 lb 2 oz) unsalted butter, softened to a spreadable consistency

1 teaspoon vanilla bean paste

sky blue gel paste food colouring

1 Follow method steps 1–3 of the Perfect Swiss Meringue Buttercream on p. 233 using the quantities given here.

2 Add enough sky blue gel paste to achieve the colour you want for the narwhal's body.

3 Cover the bowl with plastic wrap and set aside at room temperature in a cool environment until needed.

ASSEMBLY & DECORATION

100 g (3½ oz) white fondant

wooden skewer

edible gold paint or edible
   gold dust mixed into a paste
   using cake decorator's rose
   spirit (available from cake
   decorating stores) or vodka

large mermaid tail silicone
   mould (available from cake
   decorating stores)

cornflour (cornstarch), for dusting

100 g (3½ oz) light blue fondant

florist wire (or you could
   use toothpicks)

20 g (¾ oz) black fondant

20 g (¾ oz) pink fondant

small circular cookie cutters
   (mine were 4 cm/1½ inches and
   6 cm/2½ inches in diameter)

STORAGE

This cake is best enjoyed
at room temperature. It
will keep refrigerated for
up to 4 days, but please
note, depending on
your refrigerator, fondant
decorations may soften.

The cake can be made up
to 2 days in advance and
kept in an airtight container
or plastic wrap at room
temperature. It can also be
frozen (wrapped in multiple
layers of plastic wrap) for up
to 3 weeks. Swiss meringue
buttercream can be made
ahead of time (see p. 233).

1 To make the narwhal tusk, roll out two tapered ropes of white fondant. Twist the tapered ropes together to form a tusk and gently press it down onto the skewer. Allow to dry completely – around 20 minutes – before painting with edible gold paint.

2 To make the tail, dust the mermaid tail mould with cornflour and use a rolling pin to gently press the blue fondant into the mould, trimming the outside edges if needed. Place in the freezer for 15 minutes, or until firm. The fondant tail should easily release from the mould.

3 To make the narwhal's water droplets, roll light blue fondant into small balls of different sizes and taper each at one side. Gently flatten each one to form a teardrop shape. Insert florist wire or a toothpick into the tip of each teardrop.

4 Working on a cake turntable, secure the bottom of the cake onto a cake board with a small dollop of buttercream and then gently twist in place. Use an offset spatula to gently crumb-coat the cake (see p. 222) with a thin layer of frosting. Carefully smooth the side of the cake until you achieve the finish you want, then chill in the refrigerator for 10–20 minutes.

5 Apply a final coat of buttercream evenly all over the crumb-coat layer, smoothing with a small cake scraper or small flexible piece of plastic.

6 Roll out some more white fondant and use a small knife to cut out the white section of the narwhal's chest. Gently press the chest onto the cake.

7 To make the eyes and cheeks, roll out the black and pink fondant and cut the pieces to size using the circular cutters. Place the cheeks onto the cake, then attach the eyes, overlapping slightly with the cheeks (you may need a tiny amount of water on the cheeks to help the eyes stick). Form the whites of the eyes by rolling small balls of white fondant and very gently pressing flat. Use a small amount of water or sugar glue to place the whites onto the eyes.

8 To make the mouth, roll out a small amount of black fondant and use a circular cookie cutter to cut out a thin crescent shape. Place onto the cake. To make flippers, roll out some more light blue fondant and use a small knife to cut two flippers (feel free to use your creativity here, as they do not need to look like mine – which I made up anyway!). Gently press the flippers onto the cake.

9 Finally, carefully place the tail, tusk and water droplets into the cake – and TA-DA, it's the cutest narwhal cake.

Roll out two tapered ropes of white fondant, twist the ropes together to form a tusk and gently press the tusk down onto a skewer. Allow to dry before painting with edible gold paint.

To make the tail, dust the mermaid tail mould with cornflour and use a rolling pin to gently press the blue fondant into the mould. Trim the edges and freeze for 15 minutes.

To make the water droplets, roll blue fondant into small balls of different sizes and taper each at one side. Gently flatten each one to form a teardrop shape. Insert florist wire into the tip of each teardrop.

For the pink cheeks use the larger cookie cutter. For the black eyes use the smaller cutter. For the whites of the eyes, roll small balls of white fondant and gently press flat. For the black mouth, use a circular cookie cutter to cut out a thin crescent.

To make flippers, roll out light blue fondant and use a small knife to cut two flippers. Roll out white fondant and cut to shape to form the narwhal's chest.

Gently place the cheeks and eyes, chest, flippers, tail and tusk onto the iced cake. Finish by poking the water drops into the cake.

LOVE CAKE: THE WEDDING EDITION

SERVES 40

In the ancient tale of the 'Love Cake', the cake is baked as a romantic gesture to charm a prince. When I came across this enchanting concept back in 2012, I knew I had to create my own version! In this wedding-cake edition, the tanginess of strawberry and lemon Swiss meringue buttercream filling is complemented by layers of deliciously sticky spiced caramel mudcake, the sweetness of Turkish Delight and the satisfying crunch of crushed pistachios. Adorned with sweet, plump figs and striking edible flowers, this cake is sure to win hearts.

Its classic aromatic flavours are irresistible too – it's hard not to be enamoured with this exquisite cake.

• •

STRAWBERRY & LEMON SWISS MERINGUE BUTTERCREAM

2 cups (440 g) caster (superfine) sugar

12 large egg whites (pasteurised egg whites are available in cartons at most major supermarkets), chilled

750 g (1 lb 10 oz) unsalted butter, softened to a spreadable consistency

2 teaspoons vanilla bean paste

40 g (1½ oz) freeze-dried strawberry or raspberry powder (available from cake decorating stores, specialty grocers, health food stores or online)

½ cup (175 g) lemon curd (see p. 226, but store-bought is fine too)

pink gel paste food colouring (optional)

1   Follow method steps 1–3 of the Perfect Swiss Meringue Buttercream recipe on p. 233 using the quantities given here.

2   Now add the strawberry powder and lemon curd and beat until fluffy. Add the pink colouring (if using) and beat until the desired shade is achieved.

3   Cover the bowl with plastic wrap and set aside at room temperature in a cool, dry environment until needed.

SPICED CARAMEL & ALMOND MUDCAKE

600 g (1 lb 5 oz) unsalted butter, chopped into chunks

600 g (1 lb 5 oz) good quality white chocolate, chopped

2 cups (440 g) firmly packed dark brown sugar

2¾ cups (685 ml) hot water

½ cup (175 g) golden syrup or honey

1¼ tablespoons vanilla bean paste

6 large eggs, at room temperature

3 cups (450 g) self-raising flour

3 tablespoons cinnamon

2 tablespoons ground ginger

4½ cups (450 g) almond meal

1   Preheat your oven to 170°C (325°F) fan-forced. Grease a 23 cm (9 inch) round cake tin and a 15 cm (6 inch) cake tin, at least 6 cm (2½ inches) deep. Line the bases and sides with baking paper. Ensure the baking paper creates a collar around 5 cm (2 inches) higher than the cake tins to allow the cakes to rise.

2   Place the butter, chocolate, sugar, water, golden syrup and vanilla bean paste in a large, heavy-based saucepan. Stir the ingredients over medium–low heat with a silicone spatula for 5 minutes, or until the chocolate melts completely and the mixture is smooth. Set aside for at least 30 minutes to cool.

3   Transfer the melted chocolate mixture to a large mixing bowl. Add the eggs, one at a time, beating after each addition using a hand-held mixer or whisk until combined. Sift the flour and spices over the chocolate mixture and mix in until combined. Fold in the almond meal until combined.

4   Pour the cake mixture into the tins and bake for 1 hour 10 minutes– 1 hour 20 minutes for the 23 cm (9 inch) cake, and 45 minutes for the 15 cm (6 inch) cake, or until a wooden skewer inserted into the centre comes out almost clean (a few crumbs on the skewer is fine but it shouldn't come out wet). Remove the cakes from the oven and allow them to cool for at least 2 hours, before turning them out onto a baking rack to cool completely.

5   Once completely cooled, you may choose to trim the outside of the cake layers to remove any darker brown patches (this is just the sugar caramelised on the outside – it's completely up to you to decide how you'd like the naked layers to look). Using a cake leveller or a long, thin knife, carefully divide your cakes into three even layers each. Cover the cake layers in plastic wrap and set aside in the refrigerator until it's time to assemble the cake.

TIPS

You can speed up the cooling process by placing your cakes in the refrigerator, covered with a clean tea towel, for an hour or so.

You can double or triple this cake recipe to serve more people if required.

ASSEMBLY & DECORATION

½ cup (165 g) apricot jam, melted (this gives the outer layers of the cake a lovely glossy finish and helps to seal in moisture and freshness)

large piping bag fitted with a 2 cm (¾ inch) star nozzle

¾ cup (100 g) crushed pistachios, plus 1 tablespoon extra for sprinkling on top of the cake

4 cake dowels (available from cake decorating stores or online)

13 cm (5 inch) cardboard cake board

10 g (¼ oz) freeze-dried strawberry or raspberry powder (available from cake decorating stores, specialty grocers, health food stores or online)

punnet edible flowers (available from specialty grocers and online)

½ cup (70 g) Turkish delight, chopped into 5 mm–1 cm (¼–½ inch) cubes

4 fresh figs, sliced (or you could leave them whole, if you prefer)

edible gold paint or edible gold lustre mixed into a paste using cake decorator's rose spirit (available from cake decorating stores) or vodka (optional)

1 Working on a cake turntable, secure the bottom layer of the 23 cm (9 inch) cake onto a cake board with a small dollop of buttercream and then gently twist in place. Use a pastry brush to thinly cover the outside edge with melted apricot jam.

2 Next, fill the piping bag with buttercream. Starting from the outside edge and working in a spiral to the centre, pipe individual stars onto the cake layer until completely covered. Sprinkle crushed pistachios on top.

3 Repeat the process, carefully stacking the two remaining large cake layers and applying jam, buttercream and pistachios. If the buttercream filling is getting too soft in between layering, place the cake in the refrigerator for a short time to firm the cake up.

4 Once the layers for the bottom tier are assembled, it's time to prepare the placement of the top tier. I usually just estimate where the cake on top will sit but you can be more precise and mark an outline using a cake tin or a round of cardboard the same size as the next tier to be added on top. Place it in the middle of the cake and lightly mark the outline with a toothpick or a knife.

5 Take one dowel and insert it into the assembled cake inside the markings (see p. 224 for more on stacking a tiered cake). Mark the height of the cake with your thumb, take the dowel out, mark with a pen and cut with scissors or a serrated knife. Using that dowel as a guide, cut the remaining three dowels. Insert the four trimmed dowels into the cake, well inside where the next cake tier will sit, and use an offcut of dowel to push them right down into the cake.

6 Place one of the smaller cake layers on the 13 cm (5 inch) cake board and place it on top of the larger cake. Repeat steps 2–3 to fill, frost and chill the cakes until firm.

7 To finish, adorn the top of the cake with piped buttercream stars, then add the remaining crushed pistachios, a dusting of freeze-dried strawberry powder, a scattering of edible flowers, Turkish delight and figs. If you like, you could add a decadent lustre to your cake by decorating some of the figs with edible gold leaf.

TIPS

This step is optional, but particularly handy if you are going to transport your cake. To secure the cakes together and make sure the tiers won't slide off, take a big wooden dowel, slightly shorter than the cake. Sharpen one end of the dowel with a clean sharpener and, using a clean hammer, carefully drive the dowel down into all the layers until it reaches the base, using a dowel offcut to help push it all the way down. Use buttercream to mask the hole created on top as well as any gaps between the tiers.

The decorative elements I've suggested here are optional. Feel free to put your own gorgeous twist on this cake depending on how much time you have up your sleeve!

STORAGE

This cake is best served at room temperature on the day of assembly and shared with your most favourite people. Leftover cake can be stored wrapped in plastic wrap or in an airtight container for 2 days at room temperature, or up to 5 days in the refrigerator, or in the freezer for up to 3 months. Simply thaw it overnight in the fridge when ready to be snacked on.

The cake can be baked in advance and stored, wrapped in plastic wrap or in an airtight container, for up to 3 days in the refrigerator. The Swiss meringue buttercream can also be made ahead of time (see p. 233).

BLACK SESAME MARBLE CAKE

SERVES 20

This luxurious looking cake is inspired by Modernist-meets-Brutalist architectural design and was created for a fashion designer friend of mine. Black sesame seeds are the hero flavour of this cake – they have a slightly nuttier, more bitter flavour than their sweeter white equivalent, and add a satisfying amount of depth and richness to desserts. The nutty, slightly bitter paste is often paired with sweet flavours like matcha or red bean in Japan and jaggery in India. My Vietnamese aunties always loved adding sweetened roasted black sesame powder to our desserts on special occasions, so this beloved flavour has to be one of my favourites.

BLACK SESAME SPONGE CAKE

140 g (5 oz) unsalted butter, at room temperature

20 g (¾ oz) black sesame paste or black tahini (available from health food stores)

1 cup (220 g) firmly packed soft brown sugar

1½ cups (220 g) self-raising cake flour or self-raising flour, sifted

1 teaspoon vanilla extract

4 large eggs, lightly whisked, at room temperature

2 tablespoons hot water

1 Preheat the oven to 160°C (315°F) fan-forced. Grease two 18 cm (7 inch) round cake tins, at least 3 cm (1¼ inches) deep, and line the bases with baking paper.

2 Using a hand-held mixer or a stand mixer fitted with the paddle attachment, beat the butter, black sesame paste and sugar on medium for 3 minutes, or until light, pale grey and creamy. Add 2 tablespoons of the flour, then gradually add the vanilla and eggs, one at a time, beating after each addition until well combined.

3 Gently fold in the remaining flour and the hot water all at once. Divide the mixture equally between the cake tins.

4 Bake for 20–25 minutes, or until the centre of each cake springs back when lightly pressed. Remove from the oven and allow to cool for 5 minutes, before turning out onto a baking rack to cool completely. Cover and set aside until needed.

BLACK SESAME BUTTERCREAM

500 g (1 lb 2 oz) unsalted butter, softened to a spreadable consistency

20 g (¾ oz) black sesame paste or black tahini (available from health food stores)

2 cups (250 g) icing (confectioners') sugar, sifted

1 teaspoon vanilla bean paste

1 Using a hand-held mixer or a stand mixer fitted with the paddle attachment, beat the butter and black sesame paste on high speed for 10–15 minutes, or until doubled in volume and very pale grey in colour.

2 Add the icing sugar, one-third at a time, and beat until well combined and fluffy.

3 Add the vanilla and beat until combined and fluffy.

GLAZE

150 g (5½ oz) good quality white chocolate, chopped

⅔ cup (150 g) caster (superfine) sugar

100 g (3½ oz) glucose syrup

100 g (3½ oz) tinned sweetened condensed milk

10 g (¼ oz) leaf gelatine sheets, soaked for 20 minutes in iced water and drained

gel paste food colouring (I used black and white)

1   Place the white chocolate in a medium heatproof bowl and set aside.

2   Combine the sugar, glucose and 110 ml (3¾ fl oz) water in a saucepan over medium heat and bring to simmering point without stirring. Remove from the heat and stir in the condensed milk and pre-soaked gelatine.

3   Pour the hot ingredients over the white chocolate and emulsify with a stick blender (or you can mix thoroughly with a spatula/spoon), being careful not to create air bubbles.

4   Divide the glaze between two bowls and tint each one with gel colours of your choice to achieve the desired shades.

5   Place plastic wrap on the surface of each glaze colour and allow to cool to around 35°C (95°F). Once at the right temperature, use immediately. Don't fret if your glaze cools before you are able to use it. Simply gently re-heat the bowls in the microwave in 5–10 second bursts, stirring in between.

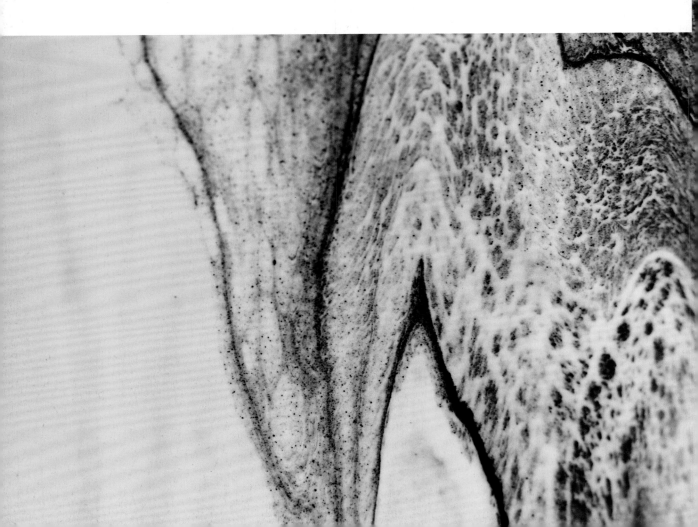

create the marbled effect, you can use the recipe for Chocolate Baubles on p. 124) or any round chocolates of your choice

see the recipe for Chocolate Baubles on p. 124

STORAGE

This kind of cake is best enjoyed at room temperature, but it will last refrigerated in an airtight container for up to 5 days.

The cake can be baked in advance and stored, wrapped in plastic wrap or in an airtight container, for up to 2 days in the refrigerator. The Swiss meringue buttercream can be made ahead of time (see p. 233). Baked cakes covered with buttercream can be covered in two layers of plastic wrap and frozen for up to 1 month. The glaze can be made ahead of time. Keep the individual colours stored separately in airtight containers in the refrigerator for up to 7 days, and when needed, gently reheat in the microwave until the correct pouring temperature is reached (35°C/95°F). Use immediately.

with a thin layer of buttercream. Chill the cake in the refrigerator for 10–20 minutes, or until firm; this will make it much easier to pipe and smooth the buttercream onto the outside.

3 Apply another layer of buttercream to the chilled cake and use a cake scraper to smooth the side (see p. 223). Finally, use an offset spatula to smooth the top of the cake by gently pulling inwards from the outer edge of the cake into the centre, cleaning the excess buttercream off the spatula with each scrape. Place in the freezer to chill for at least 1 hour.

4 Remove the cake from the freezer and gently lift it from the cake board (you can use a hot knife and a large spatula for this). Place the cake on a cooling rack or on a sturdy object slightly smaller than your cake (such as an upside-down cake tin) on top of a large baking tray (to catch the run-off glaze). *See p. 203 for step-by-step photographs.*

5 Working quickly, alternate pouring each coloured glaze onto the centre of the cake, then work your way out to the edges. Once the cake is fully covered, use a hair dryer to give the surface a quick blast (this creates a marbled effect). Let the glaze continue to drip and set for about 3 minutes.

6 Use large spatulas to carefully place the frozen cake onto a cake board. Adorn it with chocolate spheres or other round chocolates and then place into the refrigerator. Allow to thaw in the refrigerator for at least 1 hour, then leave at room temperature for at least 1 hour before serving (so your friends won't be eating firm chunks of buttercream and hard cake).

FLORAL-FEST PARTY CAKE

SERVES 16

What screams PARTY louder than entering a room full of friends with a colourfully patterned cake? Layers of buttery lemon sponge cake filled with a lip-smackingly tangy sherbet buttercream are dressed to perfection for the occasion in an eye-catching edible printed wrap with bold floral accessories. Edible printed icing is an easy and effective way to create an impressive cake. Here's everything you need to know about this well-loved technique of mine – make it your next party trick!

....

LEMON SPONGE CAKE

150 g (5½ oz) unsalted butter, at room temperature

1 cup (220 g) caster (superfine) sugar

1½ cups (220 g) self-raising cake flour or self-raising flour, sifted

1 teaspoon vanilla bean paste

2 teaspoons finely grated lemon zest

2 teaspoons lemon juice

4 large eggs, lightly whisked, at room temperature

2 tablespoons hot water

1   Preheat the oven to 160°C (315°F) fan-forced. Grease two 15 cm (6 inch) round cake tins, at least 6 cm (2½ inches) deep (each cake will be sliced into two even layers once cooled). Line the bases and sides with baking paper. Alternatively, you can bake the cakes in four 15 cm (6 inch) round single layer cake tins (in which case reduce the baking time by 5 minutes).

2   Using a hand-held mixer or a stand mixer fitted with the paddle attachment, beat the butter and sugar on medium speed for 3 minutes, or until light and fluffy. Add 2 tablespoons of the flour, then gradually add the vanilla, lemon zest and juice and beat until combined. Add the eggs one at a time, beating well after each addition.

3   Gently fold in the remaining flour and the water all at once. Divide the mixture equally between the cake tins.

4   Bake for 20–25 minutes, or until the centre of each cake springs back when lightly pressed. Remove from the oven and allow to cool for 5 minutes, before turning out onto a baking rack to cool completely. If using the standard round cake tins (rather than the single layer tins), use a cake leveller or a long, thin knife to divide the cakes into two even layers (you should have four layers in total). Cover and set aside until needed.

....

SHERBET BUTTERCREAM

500 g (1 lb 2 oz) salted butter, softened to a spreadable consistency

2 cups (250 g) icing (confectioners') sugar, sifted

1 teaspoon vanilla bean paste

100 g (3½ oz) sherbet powder

1   Using a hand-held mixer or a stand mixer fitted with the paddle attachment, beat the butter on high speed for 10–15 minutes, or until doubled in volume and very pale in colour.

2   Add the icing sugar, one-third at a time, and beat until well incorporated and fluffy.

3   Add the vanilla and beat until combined and fluffy, then fold in the sherbet until evenly distributed.

TIP   To avoid an icing-sugar explosion, I turn the mixer off to add the icing sugar and then slowly turn it back up to full speed to incorporate it.

ASSEMBLY & DECORATION

2 x A3 sheets of edible printed wafer paper, in a tropical design (available from cake decorating stores or online; you can choose pre-made designs or even submit your own for a custom print)

fresh edible flowers with food-safe stems (see p. 218 for more information on working with fresh flowers)

see p. 218

STORAGE

This cake is best served at room temperature on the day of assembly. It can be refrigerated in an airtight container for up to 1 day – any longer and the edible printed icing begins to dry out and the flowers will wilt.

The lemon sponge cake can be made up to 2 days in advance and sealed in plastic wrap at room temperature or refrigerated until needed. Edible printed paper can be made/printed up to 1 month in advance. Store it in airtight wrapping, away from moisture and sunlight (as the colours can fade).

1   Working on a cake turntable, secure the bottom layer of cake onto a cake board with a small dollop of buttercream and then gently twist in place. Use an offset spatula to spread a 1 cm (½ inch) layer of buttercream right to the edge of the cake.

2   Repeat this layering process until you have used all the cake layers, leaving the final top layer uncovered. Use an offset spatula to gently crumb-coat the cake (see p. 222) with a thin layer of frosting. Chill the cake in the refrigerator for 10–20 minutes. This will make it much easier to pipe and smooth the buttercream onto the outside.

3   Apply another layer of buttercream to the chilled cake and use a cake scraper to smooth the side (see p. 223). Finally, use an offset spatula to smooth the top of the cake by gently pulling inwards from the outer edge of the cake into the centre, cleaning the excess buttercream off the spatula with each scrape. Place in the refrigerator until needed.

4   To cover the side, use a tape measure to measure the height and circumference of your cake – be sure to allow for an overlap of 5 mm–1 cm (¼–½ inch). Use a lead pencil or pen to mark this out on the back of the edible printed paper sheet. For the cake top, trace the top of your cake tin onto the back of the edible printed paper sheet. Use a pair of scissors to cut out the shapes. ***See p. 172 for step-by-step photographs.***

5   Take the cake out of the refrigerator. Remove the backing from the edible paper for the side of the cake and carefully wrap the paper around the cake, pressing lightly. Use a very small amount of sugar glue, jam or water to seal the overlapping edge. Remove the backing for the top of the cake and position in place.

6   Using the photo as a guide (or you may want to exercise your own creativity!), artfully decorate the cake with a few fresh flowers (it's best to do this on the day of serving).

TERRAZZO MAGNIFICO

SERVES 24

Terrazzo is having a major resurgence, but in my heart it never left. I just love the unique flecks of colours and soothing stone textures – sure to impress any graphic designer or interior designer friends.

This fluffy, moist cake was created for a vegan friend of mine and I think it's the best vegan vanilla cake I've made so far. The recipe uses aquafaba, which is the liquid from a can of chickpeas (but don't worry, you can't taste it in the cake!). It acts as a binder, similar to egg whites, and you can whisk it to make meringues, fluffy mousses and more.

VEGAN VANILLA CAKE

2½ cups (625 ml) plain soy milk

1 tablespoon apple cider vinegar

1 cup (250 ml) aquafaba
  (from 2 x 425 g/15 oz
  cans chickpeas)

250 g (9 oz) softened
  vegan butter

1 cup (250 ml) canola oil
  or melted coconut oil

2½ cups (550 g) caster
  (superfine) sugar

2 tablespoons vanilla bean paste

4⅓ cups (650 g) plain
  (all-purpose) cake
  flour or plain flour

2 tablespoons baking powder

1 teaspoon sea salt

1 Preheat the oven to 170°C (325°F) fan-forced. Grease an 18 cm (7 inch) round cake tin and a 13 cm (5 inch) round cake tin. Both should be at least 8 cm (3¼ inches) deep. Line the bases and sides with baking paper. Ensure the baking paper creates a collar around 5 cm (2 inches) higher than the cake tins to allow the cakes to rise.

2 Make vegan buttermilk by combining the soy milk and apple cider vinegar. Stir a little, then set aside.

3 Using a hand-held mixer or stand mixer fitted with the whisk attachment, whisk the aquafaba in a bowl for 1 minute or until foamy and light, then set aside.

4 Using a hand-held mixer or stand mixer fitted with the paddle attachment, beat the softened vegan butter, oil and sugar together on medium speed for 2 minutes, or until creamy and well combined.

5 Measure out 1 cup (250 ml) of the whisked aquafaba and add it to the vegan butter mixture, along with the vanilla. Beat on low until well combined.

6 In a separate bowl, sift together the flour, baking powder and salt.

7 With the mixer on low speed, alternate adding the flour mixture and the vegan buttermilk, mixing after each addition until just combined. The batter should be fairly smooth (a few lumps are okay), but avoid over-mixing.

8 Pour the cake batter evenly into the prepared tins and bake for 25 minutes for the 13 cm (5 inch) cake, and 45 minutes for the 18 cm (7 inch) cake, or until the cake edges are golden brown, the surface looks and feels set and a skewer comes out mostly clean, with no wet batter.

9 Remove the tins from the oven and allow to cool for 20 minutes, before turning out onto a baking rack to cool completely. You can place them in the refrigerator to speed up the cooling process if you need to. Once cooled, use a cake leveller or a long, thin knife, to carefully divide each cake into three even layers. Cover and set aside until assembly.

VEGAN VANILLA BUTTERCREAM

500 g (1 lb 2 oz) softened vegan butter

5 cups (625 g) icing (confectioners') sugar

4–5 tablespoons unsweetened non-dairy milk

2 teaspoons vanilla bean paste

1 Using a hand-held mixer or stand mixer fitted with the paddle attachment, beat the vegan butter on high speed for 2 minutes, or until creamy.

2 Gradually add the icing sugar on low speed, ½ cup at a time, until all the sugar is thoroughly combined.

3 With the mixer on medium–low, add the non-dairy milk, 1 tablespoon at a time. Add the vanilla and increase the speed to high. Beat for about 30 seconds, or until light and fluffy.

TIP If the buttercream seems too thick, you can add more non-dairy milk, 1 tablespoon at a time. If the buttercream is too thin and runny, simply add more icing sugar, ½ cup at a time, until the desired consistency is achieved.

ASSEMBLY & DECORATION

4 x A3 sheets of edible printed wafer paper in a terrazzo design (available from cake decorating stores or online; you can choose pre-made designs or even submit your own for a custom print)

4 cake dowels (available from cake decorating stores or online)

13 cm (5 inch) cardboard cake board

1 Working on a cake turntable, secure the bottom layer of the 18 cm (7 inch) cake onto a cake board with a small dollop of buttercream and then gently twist in place.

2 Use an offset spatula to spread a 5 mm (¼ inch) layer of buttercream right to the edge of the cake. Repeat the process with the second and third layers, leaving the final top layer uncovered. Use an offset spatula to gently crumb-coat the cake (see p. 222) with a thin layer of frosting. Chill the cake in the refrigerator for 10–20 minutes; this will make it much easier to pipe and smooth the buttercream onto the outside.

3 Apply another layer of buttercream to the cake and use a cake scraper to smooth the side (see p. 223). Finally, use an offset spatula to smooth the top of the cake by gently pulling inwards from the outer edge of the cake into the centre, cleaning the excess buttercream off the spatula with each scrape. Place in the refrigerator until needed.

4 To cover the side, use a tape measure to measure the height and circumference of your cake – be sure to allow for an overlap of 5 mm–1 cm (¼–½ inch). Use a lead pencil or pen to mark this out on the back of the edible printed paper sheet. For the cake top, trace the top of your 18 cm (7 inch) cake tin onto the back of the edible printed paper sheet. Use a pair of scissors to cut out the shapes. *See p. 172 for step-by-step photographs.*

5 Take the cake out of the refrigerator. Remove the backing from the edible paper for the side of the cake and carefully wrap the paper around the cake, pressing lightly. Use a very small amount of sugar glue, jam or water to seal the overlapping edge. Remove the backing for the top of the cake and position in place.

This cake is best served at room temperature. It can be refrigerated in an airtight container for up to 1 day – any longer and the edible printed icing begins to dry out.

The vegan vanilla cake can be made up to 2 days in advance and sealed in plastic wrap at room temperature or refrigerated until needed. You can make the vegan vanilla buttercream in advance and store it in the refrigerator for 1–2 weeks. It will firm up a bit when cold, so let it warm for 30 minutes at room temperature before frosting. (If you find it is a little stiff you can briefly beat it again.) Edible printed icing can be made/printed up to 1 month in advance. Store it in an airtight container, away from moisture and sunlight (as the colours can fade).

6 Place the cake in the refrigerator to chill for at least 30 minutes.

7 Now prepare the placement of the top tier. I usually just estimate where the cake on top will sit but you can be more precise and mark an outline by using a cake tin or a round of cardboard the same size as the next tier to be added on top. Place it in the middle of the cake and lightly mark the outline with a toothpick or a knife.

8 Take one dowel and insert it into the cake inside the markings (see p. 224 for more on stacking a tiered cake). Mark the height of the cake with your thumb, take the dowel out, mark it with a pen and cut with scissors or a serrated knife. Use that dowel as a guide to cut the remaining three dowels. Insert the four trimmed dowels into the cake, well inside where the next cake tier will sit, and use a dowel offcut to push them right down into the cake.

9 Place one of the smaller cake layers on the 13 cm (5 inch) cake board. Repeat steps 2–3 to fill, frost and chill the cakes until firm.

10 To place the second tier on top of the first, use a large metal spatula or cake lifter to help carefully guide the cake into the middle, within the outline you have marked.

11 Repeat the same wrapping process using edible printed paper.

TIP This step is optional, but particularly handy if you are going to transport your cake. Before you place the top layer of edible printed paper, take a big wooden dowel, slightly shorter than the cake. Sharpen one end of the dowel with a clean sharpener and, using a clean hammer, carefully drive the dowel down into all the layers until it reaches the base, using a dowel offcut to help push it all the way down. Use buttercream to mask the hole created, then place the printed paper on top. This process helps secure the cakes together and prevents the tiers from sliding off.

For the side of the cake, use a tape measure to measure the height and circumference of each cake size – be sure to allow for a small overlap. For the cake tops, trace the top of your cake tins onto the back of the edible printed paper sheet.

Wrap the first tier in wafer paper before placing the second cake in place.

Remove the backing from the edible paper and carefully wrap the paper around the chilled cake, pressing lightly. Use a very small amount of sugar glue to seal the overlapping edge.

Remove the backing from the paper for the top of the cake and position in place.

CHOC-SPIKED PARTY STARTER

SERVES 10

This iconic cake design is not for the faint of heart! I whip it out whenever I want to create a conversation piece for the table. Inspired by black metal culture, medieval armour and brutalist architecture, this spiked chocolate cake combines so many of my favourite things. The spikes are made from white chocolate, and while the chocolate sphere looks deadly, it is hollow and is designed to adorn your cake proudly just like the star on a Christmas tree. I used banana cake filled with peanut butter Swiss meringue buttercream for this recipe, as it's sturdy enough to hold the weight of the chocolate decorations.

BANANA CAKE

1½ cups (220 g) self-raising cake flour or self-raising flour

¼ teaspoon bicarbonate of soda (baking soda)

2 cups (480 g) ripe bananas, mashed

¾ cup (165 g) firmly packed dark brown sugar

1 teaspoon vanilla extract

150 g (5½ oz) unsalted butter, at room temperature

3 large eggs, at room temperature

pinch sea salt flakes

½ cup (125 g) sour cream, at room temperature

⅔ cup (85 g) walnuts, chopped

1 Preheat the oven to 160°C (315°F) fan-forced. Grease a 15 cm (6 inch) round cake tin, at least 6 cm (2½ inches) deep, and line the base and side with baking paper.

2 In a large bowl, sift together the flour and bicarbonate of soda.

3 Using a hand-held mixer or a stand mixer fitted with the whisk attachment, whisk together the mashed banana, sugar, vanilla extract, butter, eggs and salt on medium speed for 2 minutes, until the mixture is light and creamy. Add the sour cream and whisk until just combined.

4 Fold through the flour in two batches, until all the ingredients are combined. Gently fold through the walnuts.

5 Pour the mixture into the cake tin and bake for 40 minutes, or until a wooden skewer inserted into the centre comes out clean. Remove from the oven and allow to cool for 20 minutes, before turning out onto a baking rack to cool completely.

6 Once cooled, use a cake leveller or a long, thin knife to carefully divide your cake into three even layers. Cover with plastic wrap and set aside until assembly.

PEANUT BUTTER SWISS MERINGUE BUTTERCREAM

1 cup (220 g) caster (superfine) sugar

5 large egg whites (pasteurised egg whites are available in cartons at most major supermarkets), chilled

300 g (10½ oz) unsalted butter, softened to a spreadable consistency

1 teaspoon vanilla bean paste

⅓ cup (90 g) smooth peanut butter

gel paste or oil-based food colouring (I used violet)

1 Follow method steps 1–3 of the Perfect Swiss Meringue Buttercream recipe on p. 233 using the ingredient quantities given here.

2 Place a third of the buttercream into a medium bowl. Add the peanut butter to the remaining two-thirds and beat until just combined. Use food colouring to tint the smaller bowl of buttercream to the desired shade.

3 Cover the bowls with plastic wrap and set aside at room temperature in a cool environment until needed.

CHOCOLATE SPHERE & CHOCOLATE SPIKES

400 g (14 oz) white chocolate (I use compound white chocolate for convenience)

food colouring for chocolate (I use violet oil-based colouring)

food-grade silicone or polycarbonate semisphere mould, 5 cm (2 inch) in diameter (available from cake decorating stores or online)

food-grade silicone or polycarbonate spike or stud mould (available from cake decorating stores or online)

1 Put the chocolate in a clean, dry, heatproof bowl over a saucepan of just-simmering water (the water should not touch the base of the bowl). Gently stir with a silicone spatula until melted, then tint with food colouring to the desired shade.

2 To make the chocolate sphere, fill at least two of the semispheres in the mould completely with melted chocolate. Firmly tap the mould on your bench to release any air bubbles. Use the cake scraper to scrape across the top of the mould to remove any excess chocolate. Allow the chocolate to thicken slightly (around 5–10 minutes). Lay a sheet of baking paper on the bench. Turn the mould upside-down and let the chocolate run back out onto the baking paper. Tap the side of the mould to assist the process.

3 Once the chocolate has finished dripping out, scrape again before turning the mould back up the right way. Check that you have a nice, smooth layer of chocolate on the semispheres. Turn the mould back upside-down and forcefully place it face down on a tray lined with baking paper to create a thicker rim around the inner edge of the semispheres. Set the semispheres by placing the mould in the refrigerator for at least 30 minutes.

4 Once the semispheres have set, gently remove them from the mould. Place both halves of each sphere on a warm frying pan or warm oven tray for 1 second only — any longer and they will melt too far and lose their shape! Carefully press both halves together and hold until completely set.

5 To make the chocolate spikes, reheat the remaining chocolate until melted. Use a piping bag or spoon to fill the mould cavities with melted chocolate. Tap lightly on the bench to release any air bubbles. *See p. 179 for step-by-step photographs.*

TIPS

Melting chocolate in the microwave can be a great time saver. Place the chocolate in a clean, dry, microwave-safe bowl and microwave at 50% power, stirring at 30-second intervals with a silicone spatula until melted.

If you have warm hands, wearing gloves will help prevent the chocolate from melting, or you can run your hands under cold water before handling the chocolate.

6 Place in the refrigerator for at least 30 minutes, or until the chocolate has hardened. To remove the chocolate spikes from the mould, gently flex the mould and use clean hands to pop the chocolate spikes out of the cavities.

7 To adhere the chocolate spikes onto the chocolate sphere, working one at a time, use a warm frying pan or oven tray to gently melt the bottom of each spike and then press onto the outside of the sphere. Allow each spike to set before applying the next. Repeat this process until you are happy with the number of spikes on your sphere (note: adding too many spikes may cause your chocolate decoration to sit too heavily on your cake).

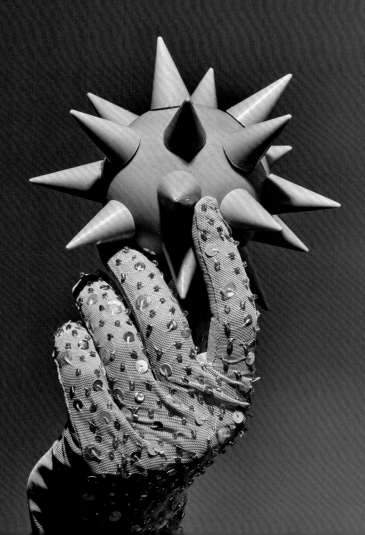

ASSEMBLY & DECORATION

1 Working on a cake turntable, secure the bottom layer of cake onto a cake board with a small dollop of buttercream and then gently twist in place. Use an offset spatula to spread a 5 mm (¼ inch) layer of peanut butter Swiss meringue buttercream right to the edge of the cake.

2 Repeat the process with the second and third layers, leaving the final top layer uncovered. If the filling gets too soft, leave it to rest in the refrigerator for at least 30 minutes to firm up to a more workable consistency.

3 Use an offset spatula to gently crumb-coat the cake (see p. 222) with a thin layer of coloured buttercream. Chill the cake in the refrigerator for 10–20 minutes; this will make it much easier to pipe and smooth the buttercream onto the outside.

4 Apply another layer of coloured buttercream to the chilled cake and use a cake scraper to smooth the side (see p. 223). Finally, use an offset spatula to smooth the top of the cake by gently pulling inwards from the outer edge of the cake into the centre, cleaning the excess buttercream off the spatula with each scrape. Do not refrigerate, as the outer buttercream needs to be slightly tacky for the chocolate spikes to embed themselves in place.

5 Using the photos as a guide (or you may choose to create your own pattern), gently embed the chocolate spikes onto the outside of the cake. Once finished, place the cake into the refrigerator for at least 1 hour to set the chocolate spikes in place. Adorn the cake with the spiked chocolate sphere once the cake is ready for its big entrance!

Use a piping bag or spoon to fill the spike mould cavities with melted chocolate and refrigerate until hardened.

When the chocolate has hardened, remove the spikes by gently flexing the mould and popping them out of the cavities.

Stick the chocolate spikes onto the chocolate sphere by melting the bottom of each spike on a warm frying pan for 1 second, then pressing onto the outside of the sphere. Allow each spike to set before applying the next.

Gently embed the chocolate spikes onto the outside of the cake.

VIBING 80S VEGAN CAKE

SERVES 20

I'm a proud kid of the 80s and the radical graphic design of this decade has always been my jam. The bold lines, squiggles and curves paired with luminous neon effects and contrasting colours are a total visual dream! Add aggressive shoulder pads, kitten heels and big hair to the mix and you've got someone who sure is ready to party. This cake was created to celebrate a dear friend's 40th birthday and she just happens to be vegan. Much like this cake, she's known for her loud accessories and effortless cool. Feel free to use your own creativity here and experiment with different colours and shapes for this distinctly 80s pattern.

CHOCOLATE CAKE

2 cups (320 g) white rice flour

1¾ cups (175 g) almond meal or almond flour

½ cup (80 g) tapioca flour

1⅔ cups (180 g) Dutch cocoa powder

1 tablespoon baking powder

1 teaspoon bicarbonate of soda (baking soda)

½ teaspoon sea salt

½ teaspoon xanthan gum

1½ cups (330 g) caster (superfine) sugar

2 cups (500 ml) plain soy milk (you could also use oat milk or any other non-dairy milk)

2 tablespoons white vinegar

¾ cup (185 ml) extra virgin olive oil

2 teaspoons vanilla bean paste

1. Preheat the oven to 165°C (320°F) fan-forced. Grease six 15 cm (6 inch) round single layer cake tins, 3 cm (1¼ inches) deep, and line with baking paper. Don't fret if you don't have enough cake tins – you can bake the cake batter in batches of two until six single layers are baked.

2. In a large mixing bowl, sift together the rice flour, almond meal, tapioca flour, cocoa powder, baking powder, bicarbonate of soda, salt and xanthan gum. Whisk to combine. Add the sugar and stir through. Make a well in the middle of your dry ingredients.

3. Add the soy milk, vinegar, 1⅔ cups (420 ml) water, olive oil and vanilla to a large jug, stirring to combine.

4. Slowly pour the wet ingredients into the dry ingredients and gently whisk to combine. It will be a runny batter.

5. Divide the batter evenly between the cake tins and firmly tap the tins on the bench to release any air bubbles.

6. Bake on two racks in your oven (rotating the tins halfway through the cooking process) for 30–40 minutes, or until a wooden skewer inserted into the centre comes out with just a few sticky moist crumbs clinging to it and the top springs back when gently touched.

7. Remove from the oven and allow to cool for 10 minutes, before turning out onto a baking rack to cool completely.

VEGAN WHITE CHOCOLATE GANACHE

1¼ cups (310 ml) plant-based cream (35% fat)

750 g (1 lb 10 oz) good quality vegan white chocolate, roughly chopped

150 g (5½ oz) vegan butter or margarine

pink natural food colouring (optional)

1   Place the cream in a large, heavy-bottomed saucepan and stir over low heat until small bubbles appear around the edge and it starts to steam. You want to catch it right before it's about to start boiling.

2   Remove from the heat and add the chocolate, making sure it is covered by the cream. Cover and let sit for 5 minutes.

3   Mix the cream and chocolate vigorously with a stick blender until smooth (you could also whisk by hand but I find a stick blender is much quicker and easier to ensure an even consistency).

4   If there are any lumps, put the pan back onto the stove over very low heat. Stir until the lumps have melted and the ganache is shiny. Alternatively, heat in the microwave in short bursts, stirring at intervals.

5   Add the butter and stir through until smooth and creamy. Tint with colouring (if using) to achieve the colour you want, stirring until evenly coloured.

6   Cover with plastic wrap, pushing it down onto the ganache surface so it covers everything. Allow it to sit for at least 1 hour (or overnight) on your bench until it has reached a smooth, slightly goopy American-style peanut butter consistency. The amount of time it will take depends on your climate. You can speed up the cooling process by placing the ganache straight into the refrigerator or even the freezer. Be sure to stir it every 20–30 minutes.

TIP You can also heat the cream using the microwave. Put the cream in a microwave-safe bowl and heat on medium (50%) for 2–3 minutes, stirring every 30 seconds, until bubbles begin to form.

ASSEMBLY & DECORATION

50 g (1¾ oz) yellow fondant

50 g (1¾ oz) pink fondant

50 g (1¾ oz) light green/
    mint fondant

50 g (1¾ oz) black fondant

50 g (1¾ oz) white fondant

50 g (1¾ oz) peach fondant

cornflour (cornstarch), for dusting

small circle cutter

2 straws (small and large)

black edible art paint
    (or edible marker)

white edible art paint
    (or edible marker)

STORAGE

This cake is best served at room temperature. Any leftovers can be refrigerated in an airtight container for up to 1 week.

You can bake the cakes 1 day in advance. Tightly cover them with plastic wrap and store at room temperature. The cakes may also be frozen for up to 2 months. Thaw them overnight in the refrigerator and gently reheat the ganache when you're ready to use it. The ganache can be prepared up to 1 week in advance and refrigerated in an airtight container. The fondant decorations can be made up to 1 month in advance. They won't be able to curve around the shape of the cake once completely dried, but will still look great! Store them in an airtight container in a cool, dark environment away from moisture.

1   Working on a cake turntable, secure the bottom layer of cake onto a cake board with a small dollop of ganache and then gently twist in place. Use an offset spatula to spread a 5 mm–1 cm (¼–½ inch) layer of ganache right to the edge of the cake. If the ganache appears too thick, gently reheat it to a more workable consistency.

2   Repeat this process until you have used all the cake layers, leaving the final top layer uncovered.

3   Use an offset spatula to gently crumb-coat the cake (see p. 222) with a thin layer of ganache (again, reheat the ganache if needed). Carefully smooth the side of the cake until you achieve the finish you want. Chill the cake in the refrigerator for 10–20 minutes; this will make it much easier to apply and smooth the ganache.

4   Apply another layer of ganache to the chilled cake and use a cake scraper to smooth the side (see p. 223). Finally, use an offset spatula to smooth the top of the cake by gently pulling inwards from the outer edge of the cake into the centre, cleaning the excess ganache off the spatula with each scrape. Place the cake in the refrigerator until needed.

5   Using the photo opposite as a guide, roll out each fondant colour to around 2 mm (¹⁄₁₆ inch) thick (I use a dusting of cornflour to prevent any stickiness). Cut into shapes using a ruler and a small, sharp knife. For the circles, I use a small circle cutter and different sized straws (again, dust with cornflour to prevent stickiness).

6   Allow the fondant shapes to dry slightly (this should take only about 20 minutes in dry conditions) and use edible art paints to decorate.

7   Now place the fondant shapes onto the cake. They should adhere to the cake on their own, but you can use a tiny dab of water if you need to. Feel free to use your own creativity with the design here; I like to layer the shapes over one another to create a graphic 80s pattern. To stick fondant shapes over one another, use a very thin layer of water as glue (but beware: less is more when it comes to water and fondant).

TIP   Instead of buying multiple colours of fondant, you can colour white fondant using different shades of gel, powdered or oil-based food colourings.

Roll out each fondant colour and cut into shapes using a ruler and a small, sharp knife. For the circles, I use a small circle cutter and different sized straws.

Allow the fondant shapes to dry slightly before using edible art paints to decorate.

Place the fondant shapes onto the iced cake.

You can layer the shapes over one another using a very thin layer of water as glue.

ROMANCE ISN'T DEAD CAKE

SERVES 16

This cake is unabashedly retro with its concentric rows of pastel buttercream, old-fashioned cursive text and glacé cherries – all in a palette worthy of Marie Antoinette. The heart shape elevates the kitsch factor, making it perfect for Galentine's Day or for gifting to anyone who believes in heart-baking cakes.

RED VELVET CAKE

1 cup (250 ml) vegetable oil

1¼ cups (275 g) caster (superfine) sugar

2 teaspoons vanilla bean paste

3 large eggs, at room temperature

2¾ cups (410 g) self-raising cake flour or self-raising flour, sifted

½ teaspoon bicarbonate of soda (baking soda)

1 tablespoon Dutch cocoa powder, sifted

1½ cups (375 ml) buttermilk, at room temperature

1 teaspoon red food colouring

1. Preheat the oven to 160°C (315°F) fan-forced. Grease a heart-shaped cake tin 20 cm (8 inches) wide and at least 8 cm (3¼ inches) deep. Line the base and side with baking paper.

2. Using a hand-held mixer or a stand mixer fitted with the whisk attachment, whisk the oil, sugar and vanilla on medium speed for 3 minutes, or until frothed. Add the eggs one at a time, whisking until just combined.

3. Mix in the flour, bicarbonate of soda and cocoa until just combined.

4. Add the buttermilk and red food colouring and mix until the batter is combined and as red as you like it, adding extra food colouring if you want a deeper shade. Be careful not to over-mix the batter.

5. Pour the batter into the cake tin and bake for 50–55 minutes, or until a wooden skewer inserted into the centre comes out clean. Remove from the oven and allow to cool for at least 20 minutes, before turning out onto a baking rack to cool completely.

6. Using a cake leveller or a long, thin knife, carefully divide your cake into two even layers.

TIP If you don't have a heart-shaped tin, you can use an 18 cm (7 inch) round cake tin instead.

RASPBERRY COMPOTE FILLING

4 cups (500 g) fresh or frozen raspberries

¾ cup (165 g) white (granulated) sugar

1 tablespoon lemon juice

2 teaspoons finely grated lemon zest

¼ cup (30 g) cornflour (cornstarch)

1   Place the frozen or fresh raspberries, white sugar, lemon juice, lemon zest and ¼ cup water in a saucepan and heat over medium–high heat. Stir the mixture until it begins to boil.

2   Lower the heat to medium–low and allow the filling to simmer for 10–15 minutes, stirring occasionally.

3   Turn the heat off and remove the saucepan from the heat. If you want a seed-free compote, pour the mixture through a metal sieve suspended over a bowl and push through using a silicone spatula. Use a decent amount of pressure to really get all the liquid through the sieve. You should be left with about ½ cup of seedy pulp which you can compost, or add a dollop to your morning granola. Or feel free to leave the seeds in if you prefer, like I have here.

4   In a separate small bowl, make a slurry by combining ¼ cup water with the cornflour. Stir until the cornflour has fully dissolved into the water. Stir this cornflour mixture into the strained raspberry compote until it is incorporated.

5   Return the compote to the saucepan and heat on medium–high heat – be sure to stir constantly during this stage to prevent it from burning. Cook until the mixture begins to boil, then reduce the heat to medium–low.

6   Continue to stir and cook for a few additional minutes. Turn the heat off and pour the compote into a bowl to cool, then cover with plastic wrap and place in the refrigerator for at least 1 hour, or preferably overnight.

PINK & RED SWISS MERINGUE BUTTERCREAM

1½ cups (330 g) caster (superfine) sugar

8 large egg whites (pasteurised egg whites are available in cartons at most major supermarkets), chilled

500 g (1 lb 2 oz) unsalted butter, softened to a spreadable consistency

1 teaspoon vanilla bean paste

pink gel paste food colouring

red gel paste food colouring

1   Follow method steps 1–3 of the Perfect Swiss Meringue Buttercream recipe on p. 233 using the ingredient quantities given here.

2   Add the pink colouring and beat until the desired shade is achieved.

3   Take out a quarter of the buttercream mixture and tint it red by mixing in the red colouring until the desired shade is achieved.

4   Cover the bowls with plastic wrap and set aside at room temperature in a cool environment until needed.

ASSEMBLY & DECORATION

medium piping bag fitted
    with a 1 cm (½ inch) tear-
    shaped (ruffling) piping tip

medium piping bag fitted with a
    3 mm (⅛ inch) circular piping tip

medium piping bag fitted with
    a 1 cm (½ inch) star tip

silver or heart-shaped cachous

10 maraschino cherries
    (available from specialty grocers)

pink chocolate or sugar bows
    (I made pink chocolate bows
    using a bow candy mould
    or you can buy these from
    cake decorating stores;
    you can also just pipe bows
    using the buttercream in the
    piping bags, if preferred)

STORAGE

This cake is best served at
room temperature. Leftovers
can be refrigerated for up to
1 week.

You can bake the cakes 1 day
in advance. Tightly cover them
with plastic wrap and store
at room temperature. The
raspberry filling can be made
up to 2 weeks in advance if
stored in an airtight container
in the refrigerator.

1   Working on a cake turntable, secure the bottom layer of cake onto
a cake board with a small dollop of buttercream and then gently
twist in place. Using the 'dam' method (see p. 221), pipe a ring of
buttercream around the edge of the cake layer, then fill the centre
with the fruit compote.

2   Place the top layer of cake on top of the compote.

3   Use an offset spatula to gently crumb-coat the cake (see p. 222) with
a thin layer of pink buttercream. Chill the cake in the refrigerator for
10–20 minutes; this will make it much easier to pipe and smooth the
buttercream onto the outside.

4   Apply another layer of buttercream to the chilled cake and use a
cake scraper to smooth the side (see p. 223). Finally, use an offset
spatula to smooth the top of the cake by gently pulling inwards from
the outer edge of the cake into the centre, cleaning the excess
buttercream off the spatula with each scrape.

5   Using a piping bag fitted with the tear-shaped piping tip, pipe pink
buttercream ruffled 'curtains' along the outside of the cake (I mark
the outline with a toothpick first to help guide me).

6   Using a piping bag fitted with the 3 mm (⅛ inch) circular piping tip,
write a message in red buttercream on top of the cake (again, mark
the text outline with a toothpick first to help guide you and then
carefully fill the outline with buttercream).

7   Use the remaining pink and red buttercream in the piping bags
fitted with the star and tear-shaped piping tips to add borders
on the side and top of the cake.

8   Finish decorating the cake using silver cachous, maraschino
cherries and pink chocolate bows.

TIP Don't worry about getting the exact type and style of the piping
tips suggested here. Use what you are able to find — all the piped
designs can be adapted. Get creative!

VINTAGE DREAMS SHOWSTOPPER

SERVES 30

Vintage buttercream-style cakes have been gaining popularity over the past few years and I personally love anything with a retro aesthetic. You may have seen them featured on cool social media accounts, online magazines and blogs but have no idea how to find a local cake artist to make one for you. Well, I'm glad you've asked, because here's how you can make your own! Vintage buttercream is so open to different variations that it makes cake decorating approachable to all – my interpretation comes with modern pastel colours and a satisfying amount of kitsch factor. The more contrasting the colours, the better!

CHOCOLATE SPONGE CAKE

FOR THE 20 CM (8 INCH) TIER

1¾ cups (260 g) self-raising cake flour or self-raising flour

½ cup (55 g) Dutch cocoa powder

280 g (10 oz) unsalted butter, at room temperature

1¼ cups (275 g) caster (superfine) sugar

5 large eggs, at room temperature

FOR THE 13 CM (5 INCH) TIER

1 cup (150 g) self-raising cake flour or self-raising flour

¼ cup (30 g) Dutch cocoa powder

140 g (5 oz) unsalted butter, at room temperature

⅔ cup (150 g) caster (superfine) sugar

3 large eggs, at room temperature

1 To bake the 20 cm (8 inch) cake tier, preheat the oven to 160°C (315°F) fan-forced. Grease two 20 cm (8 inch) round cake tins, at least 8 cm (3¼ inches) deep, and line the bases and sides with baking paper.

2 Sift together the flour and cocoa in a medium bowl.

3 Using a hand-held mixer or a stand mixer fitted with the paddle attachment, beat the butter and sugar on medium speed for 3 minutes, or until light and fluffy. Add the eggs one at a time, and beat until fluffy.

4 Fold through the sifted dry ingredients, until combined.

5 Divide the mixture evenly between the two tins. Level the surface using a spatula or the back of a spoon.

6 Bake for 30 minutes, or until the tops of the cakes spring back when gently pressed. Remove from the oven and allow to cool for 10 minutes, before carefully turning out onto a baking rack to cool completely.

7 Repeat this process to make the top tier of the cake, using two 13 cm (5 inch) round cake tins, at least 8 cm (3¼ inches) deep. Bake for 20 minutes, or until the tops of the cakes spring back when gently pressed. Remove from the oven and allow to cool for 10 minutes, before carefully turning out onto a baking rack to cool completely.

8 Once cooled, use a cake leveller or a long, thin knife to carefully divide the four cakes into two even layers each. You'll now have eight cake layers. Cover with plastic wrap and set aside until assembly.

SALTED CARAMEL SWISS MERINGUE BUTTERCREAM

3 cups (660 g) caster (superfine) sugar

16 large egg whites (pasteurised egg whites are available in cartons at most major supermarkets), chilled

900 g (2 lb) unsalted butter, softened to a spreadable consistency

1 teaspoon vanilla bean paste

310 g (11 oz) salted caramel or dulce de leche (store-bought is just fine, but you could also make your own, see p. 228 and p. 229)

teal, pink, violet and orange gel paste food colouring

1. Follow method steps 1–3 of the Perfect Swiss Meringue Buttercream recipe on p. 233 using the ingredient quantities given here.

2. Divide the buttercream into thirds. Flavour one third with the caramel/dulce de leche and thoroughly mix through.

3. Tint another third by mixing in the teal colouring until the desired shade is achieved.

4. Divide the remaining third into three smaller portions and tint each one separately: pink, violet and orange.

5. Cover the bowls with plastic wrap and set aside at room temperature in a cool environment until needed.

ASSEMBLY & DECORATION

5 cake dowels (available from cake decorating stores or online)

10 cm (4 inch) cardboard cake board

medium piping bag fitted with a 1 cm (½ inch) tear-shaped (ruffling) tip

large piping bag fitted with a 2 cm (¾ inch) star tip

medium piping bag fitted with a 1 cm (½ inch) star tip

heart-shaped silver cachous

sugared almonds

white candy-coated chocolate pearls

3 teaspoons rainbow sprinkles (I used a sprinkle mix of confetti sprinkles and rainbow jimmies)

1. Working on a cake turntable, secure the bottom layer of the 20 cm (8 inch) cake onto a cake board with a small dollop of caramel buttercream and then gently twist in place.

2. Use an offset spatula to spread a 5 mm (¼ inch) layer of caramel buttercream right to the edge of the cake.

3. Repeat the process with the remaining 20 cm (8 inch) cake layers, leaving the final top layer uncovered. If the buttercream filling is getting too soft in between layering, place the cake in the refrigerator for a short time to firm the cake up and provide stability (you may have to do this a few times).

4. Use an offset spatula to gently crumb-coat the cake (see p. 222) with a thin layer of the teal buttercream. Chill the cake in the refrigerator for 10–20 minutes; this will make it much easier to pipe and smooth the buttercream onto the outside.

5. Apply another layer of teal buttercream to the chilled cake and use a cake scraper to smooth the side (see p. 223). Finally, use an offset spatula to smooth the top of the cake by gently pulling inwards from the outer edge of the cake into the centre, cleaning the excess ganache off the spatula with each scrape. Place the cake in the refrigerator until it is chilled, at least 1 hour, as it is much easier to work with a chilled cake with firm frosting.

6   Once the layers for the bottom tier are assembled, it's time to prepare the placement of the top tier. I usually just estimate where the cake on top will sit but you can be more precise and mark an outline by using a cake tin or a round of cardboard the same size as the smaller tier. Place it in the middle of the cake and lightly mark the outline with a toothpick or a knife.

7   Take one dowel and insert it into the cake inside the markings (see p. 224). Mark the height of the cake with your thumb, take the dowel out, mark it with a pen and cut with scissors or a serrated knife. Use that dowel as a guide to cut the remaining three dowels. Insert the four trimmed dowels into the cake, well inside where the next cake tier will sit, and use a dowel offcut to push them right down into the cake.

8   Place one of the smaller cake layers on the 10 cm (4 inch) cardboard cake board. Repeat steps 3–5 to fill, frost and chill the cakes until firm.

9   To place the second tier on top of the first, use a large metal spatula or cake lifter to help carefully guide the cake into the middle, within the outline you have marked.

10   This step is optional, but particularly handy if you are going to transport or carry your cake. To secure the cakes together and make sure the tiers won't slide off, take a big wooden dowel, slightly shorter than the cake. Sharpen one end of the dowel with a clean sharpener and, with the help of a clean hammer, carefully drive it down into all the layers until it reaches the base, using a dowel offcut to help push it all the way down. Use buttercream to mask the hole on top as well as cover any gaps or blemishes between the tiers.

11   Using a medium piping bag fitted with a 1 cm (½ inch) ruffling tip, pipe pink buttercream ruffled 'curtains' along the outside of both tiers of the cake (I mark the outline with a toothpick first to help guide me). *See p. 196 for step-by-step photographs.*

12   Using a large piping bag fitted with a 2 cm (¾ inch) star piping tip, pipe a violet buttercream border along the bottom of each tier and the top of the upper tier.

13   Using a medium piping bag fitted with a 1 cm (½ inch) star tip, fill in the remaining orange buttercream borders.

14   Finish decorating the cake using silver cachous, sugared almonds and candy-coated chocolate pearls.

15   Decorate the top of the cake (inside the top circular buttercream border) with rainbow sprinkles.

Start by piping pink buttercream ruffled 'curtains' along the outside of the cake on both the top and bottom tiers (I mark the outline with a toothpick first to help guide me).

Using a large star piping tip, pipe a violet buttercream border along the bottom of each tier and the top of the upper tier.

Using the small star tip, fill in the remaining orange buttercream borders.

Finish decorating the cake using silver cachous, sugared almonds and candy-coated chocolate pearls.

GALAXY GLAZE CAKE

SERVES 16–20

The planets, the stars, the crazy colours, UFOs, the final frontier – everything about the universe is exciting! As a fully fledged adult I am obsessed with space. This cake is guaranteed to impress all your favourite science-nerd friends, as it boasts a clever cake-decorating technique that will take your skills into outer space. The glossy mirror glaze finish is a traditional technique used to decorate mousse cakes (known as entremets) and pastries. Giving the glaze a quick blast of heat with a hair dryer creates a smooth, out-of-this-world effect, reminiscent of the flashes of metallic colour and light seen in faraway galaxies.

DARK CHOCOLATE SEA SALT CAKE

2½ cups (370 g) self-raising cake flour or self-raising flour, sifted

1½ cups (330 g) caster (superfine) sugar

½ cup (55 g) Dutch cocoa powder, sifted

½ teaspoon bicarbonate of soda (baking soda)

½ teaspoon sea salt

150 g (5½ oz) dark chocolate, chopped

1 cup (250 ml) coconut oil

4 large eggs, at room temperature

1½ cups (375 ml) milk, at room temperature

1 teaspoon vanilla extract

1. Preheat the oven to 160°C (315°F) fan-forced. Grease three 18 cm (7 inch) round cake tins, at least 3 cm (1¼ inches) deep, and line the bases and sides with baking paper.

2. In a large bowl or the bowl of a stand mixer, gently fold together the dry ingredients until combined.

3. Put the dark chocolate and coconut oil in a clean, dry, heatproof bowl over a saucepan of just-simmering water (the water should not touch the base of the bowl). Gently stir with a silicone spatula until melted, then set aside to cool to room temperature.

4. Using a hand-held mixer or stand mixer fitted with the paddle attachment, slowly add the chocolate mixture to the dry ingredients and beat on low speed until just combined. Beat in the eggs, one at a time, followed by the milk and vanilla extract. Mix until combined, being careful not to over-mix.

5. Divide the batter evenly between the prepared cake tins and bake for 45 minutes, or until a wooden skewer inserted into the centre comes out clean. Remove from the oven and allow to cool in the tins for at least 1 hour, before turning out onto a baking rack to cool completely.

TIP Melting chocolate in the microwave can be a great time saver. Place the chocolate and coconut oil in a clean, dry, microwave-safe bowl and microwave at 50% power, stirring at 30-second intervals with a silicone spatula until melted.

DARK CHOCOLATE BUTTERCREAM

1½ cups (330 g) caster (superfine) sugar

8 large egg whites (pasteurised egg whites are available in cartons at most major supermarkets), chilled

300 g (10½ oz) good quality dark chocolate, chopped

500 g (1 lb 2 oz) unsalted butter, softened to a spreadable consistency

1 teaspoon vanilla bean paste

1 Place the sugar and egg whites in a heatproof glass bowl. Set the bowl over a saucepan of just-simmering water (the water should not touch the base of the bowl), and whisk until the sugar has dissolved and the egg whites are slightly warm to the touch (at least 40°C/104°F). (You can omit this step entirely if you are using pasteurised egg whites, and instead, simply place the sugar and egg whites directly into the mixer.)

2 Transfer the mixture into the bowl of a stand mixer. Using the whisk attachment, whisk on high speed until the mixture has formed stiff and glossy peaks, around 10–15 minutes.

3 Meanwhile, put the dark chocolate in a clean, dry, heatproof bowl over a saucepan of just-simmering water (the water should not touch the base of the bowl). Gently stir with a silicone spatula until melted. Remove from the heat and allow to cool slightly.

4 Switch to the paddle attachment on your stand mixer. Add the butter to the egg whites, in thirds, and beat on high speed after each addition until incorporated. Don't be alarmed if the buttercream appears curdled – it will become light and fluffy once whisked for around 2–5 minutes (I absolutely promise!). Beat in the melted chocolate and add the vanilla. Continue to beat until fluffy, and then beat on low speed to eliminate air bubbles.

5 Cover the bowl with plastic wrap and set aside at room temperature in a cool environment until needed.

TIP Melting chocolate in the microwave can be a great time saver. Place the chocolate in a clean, dry, microwave-safe bowl and microwave at 50% power, stirring at 30-second intervals with a silicone spatula, until melted.

GLAZE

150 g (5½ oz) good quality white chocolate, chopped

⅔ cup (150 g) caster (superfine) sugar

100 g (3½ oz) glucose syrup

100 g (3½ oz) tinned sweetened condensed milk

12 g (¼ oz) leaf gelatine sheets soaked for 20 minutes in iced water and drained

gel paste food colours (I used black, purple and blue)

1 Place the white chocolate in a medium heatproof bowl and set aside.

2 Combine the sugar, glucose and 110 ml (3¾ fl oz) water in a medium saucepan over medium heat and bring to the boil without stirring. As soon as it boils, remove the saucepan from the heat. Stir the sweetened condensed milk and pre-soaked gelatine through the sugar syrup.

3 Pour the hot ingredients over the white chocolate and emulsify with a stick blender (or you can mix thoroughly with a spatula/spoon), being careful not to create air bubbles.

4 Divide the glaze between three bowls and tint with the gel colours to the desired shades.

5 Place plastic wrap on the surface of each glaze colour and allow to cool to around 35°C (95°F). Once at the right temperature, use immediately. Don't fret if your glaze cools before you are able to use it. Simply gently re-heat the bowls in the microwave in 5–10 second bursts, stirring in between.

ASSEMBLY & DECORATION

hair dryer at the ready!

edible metallic rock candy
   (available from cake decorating
   stores and online)

small food-safe paint brush

edible silver paint or edible
   silver lustre mixed into a paste
   using cake decorator's rose
   spirit (available from cake
   decorating stores) or vodka

edible star sprinkles

1 Working on a cake turntable, secure the bottom layer of cake onto
a cake board with a small dollop of chocolate buttercream and then
gently twist in place. Use an offset spatula to spread a 5 mm (¼ inch)
layer of buttercream right to the edge of the cake.

2 Repeat the process with the second and third layers, leaving the
final top layer uncovered.

3 Use an offset spatula to gently crumb-coat the cake (see p. 222)
with a thin layer of buttercream. Chill the cake in the refrigerator
for 10–20 minutes; this will make it much easier to apply and smooth
the buttercream onto the outside.

4 Apply another layer of buttercream to the chilled cake and use a
cake scraper to smooth the side (see p. 223). Finally, use an offset
spatula to smooth the top of the cake by gently pulling inwards from
the outer edge of the cake into the centre, cleaning the excess
buttercream off the spatula with each scrape. Place the cake in the
freezer to chill for at least 1 hour.

5 Remove the frozen cake from the freezer and gently lift it from the
cake board (you can use a hot knife and a large spatula for this).
Place the cake on a sturdy object slightly smaller than your cake
(such as an upside-down cake tin) on top of a large baking tray
(to catch the run-off glaze).

6 Working quickly, alternate pouring each coloured glaze onto
different areas of the cake (see opposite). Once the cake is fully
covered, use a hair dryer to give the surface a quick blast to create
a marbled effect. Let the glaze continue to drip and set for about
3 minutes.

7 Use large spatulas to carefully place the finished frozen cake onto
a cake board. Decorate the bottom edge of the cake with edible
metallic rock candy. Use a clean food-safe paint brush to lightly
splatter edible silver paint over the cake to create a galaxy of stars
(you can practise on a piece of paper or paper towel first) and then
finish with a sprinkling of edible stars.

8 Place the cake into the refrigerator. Allow it to thaw there for at least
1 hour, then leave it at room temperature for at least 1 hour before
serving (so your friends won't be eating firm chunks of buttercream
and hard cake).

Place the cake on a sturdy object slightly smaller than your cake (such as an upside-down cake tin) on top of a large baking tray (to catch the run-off glaze).

Working quickly, alternate pouring each coloured glaze onto different areas of the cake.

Once the cake is fully covered, use the hair dryer to give the surface a quick blast to create a marbled effect.

Decorate the base of the cake with some edible metallic rock candy. Use a food-safe paint brush to lightly splatter silver edible paint over the cake to create a galaxy of stars, then finish with a sprinkling of edible stars.

HAZELNUT MERINGUE CELEBRATION TORTE

SERVES 20

This hazelnut meringue torte is a smaller (but equally divine) version of my best friend Milena's wedding cake. We've been besties for almost 25 years, so when she asked me to be her maid of honour, you know I was enthusiastically all over the dessert preparations! She wanted something less traditional than the flour-based white wedding cake and is a huge fan of contrasting textures and Italian desserts. We decided to go with the divine combination of luscious chocolate mousse sandwiched between alternating layers of chewy chocolate and date meringue and hazelnut japonaise.

....

CHOCOLATE DATE MERINGUE DISCS

6 large egg whites (pasteurised egg whites are available in cartons at most major supermarkets), chilled

½ teaspoon cream of tartar

1 cup (220 g) caster (superfine) sugar

2 cups (280 g) Brazil nuts, coarsely chopped

200 g (7 oz) pitted dates, coarsely chopped into 1 cm (½ inch) pieces

150 g (5½ oz) good quality dark chocolate, coarsely chopped

50 g (1¾ oz) good quality milk chocolate, coarsely chopped

1 Preheat the oven to 120°C (235°F) fan-forced. Grease two 23 cm (9 inch) round cake tins and line with baking paper.

2 Using a hand-held mixer or a stand mixer fitted with the whisk attachment, whisk the egg whites with the cream of tartar on medium–high speed for 2–3 minutes, or until firm peaks form. Gradually add the caster sugar and continue whisking on high speed for 2–3 minutes, or until the sugar dissolves. Fold the chopped Brazil nuts, dates and chocolate through the meringue using a spatula until combined.

3 Divide the meringue mixture between the two cake tins and use the back of a spoon to smooth the surface.

4 Place the cake tins in the oven and immediately reduce the oven temperature to 100°C (200°F). Bake for around 60 minutes (rotating the cake tins halfway through cooking), or until lightly coloured. Turn the oven off and leave the meringues in the oven with the door ajar to cool to room temperature.

TIP When making meringues, make sure that both the mixing bowl and the whisk are clean and dry, as any moisture or fat will stop the egg whites from forming a meringue. It is also important to add the sugar slowly or the meringue will collapse.

HAZELNUT JAPONAISE

8 large egg whites (pasteurised egg whites are available in cartons at most major supermarkets), at room temperature

2 cups (440 g) caster (superfine) sugar

2 cups (220 g) hazelnut meal

1 Preheat the oven to 120°C (235°F) fan-forced. Grease two 23 cm (9 inch) round cake tins and line with baking paper.

2 Using a hand-held mixer or a stand mixer fitted with the whisk attachment, whisk the egg whites on medium speed for 2 minutes, or until soft peaks form. Gradually add the caster sugar and continue whisking on high speed for 2–3 minutes, or until the sugar dissolves. Fold in the hazelnut meal until just combined.

3 Divide the mixture between the two cake tins and use the back of a spoon to smooth the surface.

4 Bake for around 2 hours (rotating the cake tins halfway through cooking), or until dry and crisp. Turn the oven off and leave the hazelnut japonaise discs in the oven with the door ajar to cool to room temperature.

MILK CHOCOLATE MOUSSE FILLING

650 g (1 lb 7 oz) good quality milk chocolate, coarsely chopped

2 cups (500 ml) thick (double) cream, plus 1⅔ cups (420 ml) extra

½ teaspoon vanilla bean paste

1 Place the chocolate in a heatproof bowl.

2 Put the 2 cups (500 ml) cream and the vanilla bean paste in a saucepan over medium heat and bring to simmering point.

3 Pour the hot cream over the chocolate and whisk until the chocolate melts and you have created a smooth mousse. Allow it to cool to the touch – around 25°C (77°F) – but not so far that it sets.

4 In a separate bowl, whip the extra cream to medium peaks (when you lift out the whisk the peaks should bend over at the tips), then fold it through the mousse until combined. Cover and set aside in the refrigerator until needed.

ASSEMBLY & DECORATION

chocolate hearts (you can pipe your own onto baking paper using melted dark chocolate, or they are available from supermarkets and cake decorating stores)

edible gold lustre (available from cake decorating stores)

handful of chopped Brazil nuts

1 teaspoon icing (confectioners') sugar, sifted, for dusting (optional)

1 To assemble, place one of the chocolate date meringue discs on your chosen plate, then take a quarter of the prepared milk chocolate mousse filling and spread it evenly over the meringue disc using a palette knife.

2 Layer with a disc of hazelnut japonaise and repeat the alternating process until all the discs are layered with the milk chocolate mousse filling. Place the remaining mousse filling on top of the fourth disc.

3 Dust some of the chocolate hearts with edible gold lustre. Decorate the top of the cake with a combination of dark chocolate hearts and gold hearts and a scattering of chopped Brazil nuts. Dust with icing sugar just before serving, if using.

STORAGE

This cake is best eaten on the day of assembly – if eaten as soon as it's assembled, you can appreciate the contrast between the crunchy meringue and the soft mousse. It can be stored in an airtight container in the refrigerator for up to 2 days – the leftovers are equally delicious and easier to cut as the chocolate mousse seeps into the meringue.

The chocolate date meringue discs and hazelnut japonaise discs can be made and stored at room temperature in an airtight container for 1 week before assembly.

CRYSTAL FLOWER CAKE

SERVES 16-20

When I planned this cake in my head, I wanted to create something beautiful, whimsical and delicate enough to sit among a tablescape of fresh flowers at an engagement party, wedding or significant birthday. To create maximum effect with relatively minimum effort, I imagined delicate flowers suspended in sugar, sitting prettily like edible jewels. The easiest part is, you're essentially just melting lollies! I've used my beloved orange poppy seed cake here for its divine fragrance and deliciously moist crumb.

ORANGE POPPY SEED CAKE

220 g (7¾ oz) unsalted butter, at room temperature

1 cup (220 g) caster (superfine) sugar

8 large eggs, at room temperature

3½ cups (350 g) almond meal

⅓ cup (60 g) poppy seeds

finely grated zest and juice of 1 large orange

2 teaspoons vanilla bean paste

1¾ cups (260 g) self-raising cake flour or self-raising flour, sifted

1   Preheat the oven to 160°C (315°F) fan-forced. Grease two 16 cm (6 inch) round cake tins, at least 8 cm (3¼ inches) deep, and line the bases and sides with baking paper. Alternatively, you could use five 16 cm (6 inch) round single layer cake tins, 3 cm (1¼ inches) deep.

2   Using a hand-held mixer or stand mixer fitted with the paddle attachment, beat the butter and caster sugar on medium speed for 3 minutes, or until light and creamy. Add the eggs one by one, beating well after each addition.

3   Gently fold in the almond meal, poppy seeds, orange zest and juice, vanilla and flour, and mix until just combined.

4   Spoon the mixture evenly into the cake tins and bake for 50–60 minutes (40 minutes if you're using five shallow cake tins), or until the top of the cakes are lightly golden. Remove from the oven and allow to cool for 20–30 minutes before turning out onto a baking rack to cool completely. Use a cake leveller or a long, thin knife to carefully divide the cakes into three even layers (skip this step if using five shallow cake tins).

CRYSTAL FLOWERS

circular silicone candy mould

500 g (1 lb 2 oz) packet clear or coloured hard lollies (candies)

dried, pressed edible flowers (see p. 231 or buy online)

1   Preheat the oven to 120°C (235°F) fan-forced. Place the silicone mould on a baking sheet.

2   Place one or two lollies in each cavity. If you are unsure how much candy your mould will hold, try melting one lolly first, then adding a second and melting again. I found one lolly was enough for the small mould I used for this cake. **See p. 215 for step-by-step photographs.**

3   Place the baking sheet and mould in the oven and bake for 15–20 minutes, or until the hard lollies have melted completely.

4   Once the lollies have melted, carefully remove the mould from the oven and use a pair of tweezers to place a flower on each one before the lollies harden. You can also use sugar glue if the lollies set too quickly.

5   Allow the flower lollies to cool and harden completely – around 30 minutes – before gently popping them out of their moulds.

WHITE CHOCOLATE SWISS MERINGUE BUTTERCREAM

1½ cups (330 g) caster (superfine) sugar

8 large egg whites (pasteurised egg whites are available in cartons at most major supermarkets), chilled

500 g (1 lb 2 oz) good quality white chocolate, chopped

500 g (1 lb 2 oz) unsalted butter, softened to a spreadable consistency

1 teaspoon vanilla bean paste

1 Place the sugar and egg whites in a heatproof glass bowl. Set the bowl over a saucepan of just-simmering water, and whisk until the sugar has dissolved and the egg whites are slightly warm to the touch (at least 40°C / 104°F). (You can omit this step entirely if you are using pasteurised egg whites, and instead, simply place the sugar and egg whites directly into the mixer.)

2 Using a hand-held mixer or a stand mixer fitted with the whisk attachment, whisk the mixture on high speed for 10–15 minutes, or until stiff, glossy peaks form.

3 Put the chocolate in a clean, dry, heatproof bowl over a saucepan of just-simmering water (the water should not touch the base of the bowl). Gently stir with a silicone spatula until melted. Remove from the heat and keep warm.

4 Add the butter, in thirds, beating on high speed after each addition until incorporated. Don't be alarmed if the buttercream appears curdled – it will become light and fluffy once beaten for around 2–3 minutes (I absolutely promise!).

5 Beat in the melted chocolate and add the vanilla. Continue to whisk until fluffy and then beat on low speed to eliminate air bubbles.

6 Cover the bowl with plastic wrap and set aside at room temperature in a cool environment until needed.

TIP To melt chocolate in the microwave, place the chocolate in a clean, dry, microwave-safe bowl and microwave at 50% power, stirring at 30-second intervals with a silicone spatula until melted.

ASSEMBLY & DECORATION

STORAGE

This cake is best enjoyed at room temperature on the day of assembly. It can be stored in an airtight container in the fridge for up to 5 days or frozen for up to 2 months. Let it come to room temperature again before serving.

The cakes can be baked ahead of time and refrigerated (wrapped in plastic) in an airtight container for up to 2 days or frozen for up to 1 month. Leave them to thaw in the fridge overnight before decorating. The buttercream can be made ahead (see p. 233), as can the crystal flower lollies, which will last for up to 2 weeks when stored in an airtight container in a cool, dry environment (to keep them from getting too sticky).

1. Working on a cake turntable, secure the bottom layer of cake onto a cake board with a small dollop of the white chocolate buttercream and then gently twist in place. Use an offset spatula to spread a 5 mm (¼ inch) layer of buttercream right to the edge of the cake.

2. Repeat this process until you have used all the cake layers, leaving the final top layer uncovered (you will have five or six layers, depending on the tins you used).

3. Use an offset spatula to gently crumb-coat the cake (see p. 222) with a thin layer of buttercream. Chill the cake in the refrigerator for 10–20 minutes; this will make it much easier to smooth the buttercream onto the outside.

4. Apply another layer of buttercream to the chilled cake and use a cake scraper to smooth the side (see p. 223). Finally, use an offset spatula to smooth the top of the cake by gently pulling inwards from the outer edge of the cake into the centre, cleaning the excess buttercream off the spatula with each scrape. Place the cake in the refrigerator until needed.

5. Artfully decorate the cake with an arrangement of crystal flowers by pressing them gently into the cake. It's best to do this on the day of the special occasion.

Place one or two lollies in each cavity; the small moulds I've used here work best with one lolly.

Place the baking sheet and mould in the oven and bake for 15–20 minutes, or until the hard lollies have melted completely.

Once the lollies have melted, carefully remove the mould from the oven and use a pair of tweezers to place a flower on each lolly before they harden. (You can also use sugar glue if the lollies begin setting too quickly.)

Allow the crystal flower lollies to cool and harden completely (around 30 minutes) before gently popping them out of their moulds.

CHAPTER 4

essential
elements

WORKING WITH FRESH FLOWERS ON CAKES

Talk to your florist about which flowers are safe to use on cakes, as some flowers are naturally toxic for consumption and others may be harmful because of pesticide use.

If in doubt, stick with any flower that is sold as an edible garnish (available from specialty grocers, online and at farmers' markets). Flowers that are edible include roses, gardenias, pansies, violets and dandelions.

It is not a requirement that the flowers need to be edible in order to use them as a cake decoration, but do be sure to remove non-edible flowers and their foliage before serving the cake.

To prepare flowers for decoration, wash them thoroughly and pat dry with a paper towel. Strip the flowers of most of their leaves and remove any large thorns or spikes. Cut the flower stems so that they are only 4 cm (1½ inches) long.

Wrap the stems tightly and thoroughly in florist's tape (this should be done for each single stem or your group of flowers). You can even dip the stems in edible food seal (available from cake decorating stores, florists and online) after they've been wrapped, for extra protection. Be mindful when inserting multiple wrapped stems into a cake – the extra bulk can cause the buttercream to bulge or crack your cake.

You can create thinner and flexible food-safe stems for your fresh flowers by cutting off the stem 1–2 cm (½–¾ inches) from the head of each flower. Insert a thin 20 cm (8 inch) length of florist wire through the base of the flower head and then fold the wire in half. Next, twist the two wire halves together to create a single wire stem for the flower. Wrap the wire stem tightly and thoroughly in florist's tape.

CUTTING, FILLING & FROSTING

The first step to making a layered cake is to cut the cake into nice, even layers (unless, of course, you've baked the cake in separate layers). The second step is to layer the cake with the filling. Once you've added the final cake layer, check that your cake is straight and level – feel free to push and manipulate the cake layers so that they are as close to straight as possible. Then it's time for the crumb-coat – a thin layer of frosting that traps the crumbs inside so that the final coat of frosting is clean and smooth. Last of all, the final layer of frosting is applied and smoothed until you're happy with the finish – whether that's a completely smooth look or a more rustic style.

CUTTING THE CAKE INTO LAYERS

Place the cake on a cake turntable. If you want the finished cake to have a nice flat top with sharp edges you may need to level the top of the cake first. If so, use a cake leveller or a long, thin knife to cut the very top of the cake flat (you can freeze the offcuts to make cake pops another time). Alternatively, divide the cake into two or three even layers and use the top layer, which may be a little rounded, on the bottom layer of your cake. You can fill any gaps with buttercream later. If you feel like you need some extra guidance, you can use a ruler to work out where you need to cut the layers and mark the spot with some toothpicks around the perimeter of the cake.

FILLING THE CAKE: BASIC LAYERING

Secure the bottom layer of cake onto a cake board with a small dollop of buttercream, and gently twist to secure it in place.

Use an offset spatula to spread a 5 mm (¼ inch) layer of buttercream right to the edge of the cake.

FILLING THE CAKE: THE 'DAM' METHOD

When using a filling you can use the 'dam' method: with a piping bag, pipe a ring of buttercream around the edge of the cake layer. This acts as a wall to prevent your filling from escaping.

Fill the buttercream 'dam' with the filling of your choice, then add the next layer of cake and continue filling and layering.

CRUMB-COATING THE CAKE

Using an offset spatula, fill in any gaps between the layers with frosting, then add several dollops of frosting towards the base of the cake and spread it up the side and over the top of the cake. The goal is to create a thin layer of frosting that completely coats the cake – it doesn't need to be perfectly smooth. Once completed, chill the cake in the refrigerator for 10–20 minutes.

ADDING THE FINAL LAYER OF FROSTING

Apply the frosting as for the crumb-coat, starting with several dollops of frosting around the base, then continue adding and spreading the frosting until there is an even layer all over. Make sure there is enough buttercream to make a substantial top layer – it still doesn't need to be completely smooth at this stage, just relatively even.

SMOOTHING THE SIDE & TOP

Hold a cake scraper parallel to the cake and rotate the turntable with your free hand, cleaning the cake scraper after every few spins. Repeat until smooth, filling in any gaps with extra frosting.

Finally, use an offset spatula to smooth the top of the cake by gently pulling inwards from the outer edge of the cake, pulling the 'lip' of excess frosting towards the centre, cleaning the excess buttercream off the spatula with each scrape.

TIP Now that you have your beautifully iced cake ready, you'll want to transfer it to a cake stand or serving plate (either from a turntable or from a cake board). Gently run a clean offset spatula all around the base of the cake to release it, then carefully slide the spatula underneath the cake and lift. You can even use a large barbecue spatula to help with this. I highly recommend that you chill the cake until firm in the refrigerator or freezer before moving it – it makes the whole process much easier, and helps prevent blemishes appearing on the buttercream.

HOW TO STACK A TIERED CAKE

Do you have a fear of the tier? Don't worry, I'm here to help – making a simple tiered cake need not be daunting! The most important thing to remember when constructing a tiered (also known as stacked) cake is SUPPORT. The cake needs adequate support to ensure that it won't sink into a bulging heap. There are different kinds of dowels that can be used to support a cake, such as wooden cake dowels, hollow plastic dowels, sturdy plastic straws and even wooden skewers. Whatever you choose, it needs to be food-safe.

My personal preference when building a tiered cake is to use wooden cake dowels. They can be found in cake decorating stores and are sturdy yet inexpensive. The tiered cake sizes I usually make are 23 cm (9 inches), 18 cm (7 inches) and 13 cm (5 inches). Of course, you can use different sizes according to your requirements – and how much you are physically able to lift!

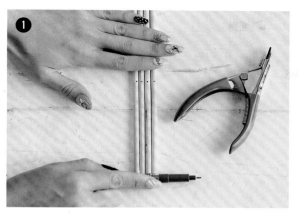

Mark the height of the dowels and trim them using clippers, small branch pruners or dowel cutters.

Insert the four trimmed dowels into the cake, well inside where the next cake tier will sit, and use a spare cake dowel or an offcut to push them right down into the cake.

Add cake dowels to the second cake tier (if your cake has more than two tiers), then carefully lift the second tier (including the cardboard cake board) on top of the first tier using a metal spatula or a cake lifter.

Use a large offset spatula to help gently slide the second cake tier off the cake lifter and into position in the centre of the first cake tier.

To make sure the tiers won't slide off, sharpen one end of a long wooden dowel with a clean pencil sharpener – make the dowel slightly shorter than the cake. Then drive the dowel down through all the cake layers.

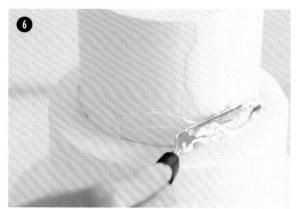

Mask the hole created on top of the cake, as well as any other gaps or blemishes between the tiers, with an offset spatula and a little left-over frosting. Finish decorating the cake as desired.

Remember to pick out the dowels after cutting, or let your cake receiver or venue know that there are dowels in the cake.

MAKE IT YOURSELF

There's something so deeply satisfying about making an utterly delicious treat from scratch. And while store-bought is absolutely fine, when you make your own you know exactly what's going into your food and the mouths of your loved ones. An added benefit is that you can tailor everything to suit your tastes – I never find store-bought lemon curd or salted caramel quite as decadent as the versions I make myself.

DIY LEMON CURD

MAKES 3 CUPS (750 ML)

While I encourage convenience where possible (some store-bought brands of lemon curd are fantastic!), homemade lemon curd always seems the most vibrant in flavour and luscious in texture. It's also a great way to reduce the number of egg yolks wasted when making meringue. I spread lemon curd on toast, stir it through yoghurt, dollop it on pancakes and use it to fill layered cakes.

2 large eggs

6 large egg yolks

finely grated zest of 2 lemons

1 cup (250 ml) strained fresh lemon juice

1 cup (220 g) caster (superfine) sugar

175 g (6 oz) unsalted butter, chopped

1   Whisk the eggs and yolks in a small non-reactive saucepan until combined. Whisk in the lemon zest, juice and sugar. Add the butter.

2   Place the pan over medium heat and whisk, scraping the bottom and side of the pan, for around 5 minutes, or until the butter is melted and the mixture is thickened and beginning to simmer around the edge. Continue whisking for a further 10 seconds. Remove the saucepan from the heat.

3   Scrape the lemon curd into a strainer set over a bowl to remove the lemon zest, if you wish. Allow the curd to cool, then chill in the refrigerator before using.

TIP   Place a piece of plastic wrap directly on top of the curd so that a skin doesn't form.

STORAGE

Lemon curd can be stored in an airtight container and refrigerated for up to 1 week.

CAKE FLOUR

MAKES 3 CUPS

I use cake flour in my baking where a fluffy texture is desirable, such as a sponge cake, vanilla cake, or any cake that you would prefer to have a light, delicate crumb.

Cake flour is low in protein, meaning less gluten, and its structure allows for the softest texture compared to other flours when used in baking.

Plain (all-purpose) flour, on the other hand, has a slightly higher protein content, meaning more moderate gluten development. It is suitable in all baking, but you will notice the difference in softness when it is used in sponge cakes rather than cake flour (which will create a fluffier sponge cake).

Bread flour contains the highest level of protein, meaning more gluten formation, and it develops the hardest texture when baked. Bread flour, is of course, perfect for bread and any other baked good that requires a firmer structure.

For convenience, I usually buy my cake flour (you can find cake flour in most supermarkets in the baking aisle next to the plain flour), but if you want to make your own it's very simple.

for plain (all-purpose) cake flour: sift 2⅔ cups (430 g) plain (all-purpose) flour with ⅓ cup (50 g) cornflour (cornstarch)

for self-raising cake flour: sift 2⅔ cups (430 g) plain (all-purpose) flour with ⅓ cup (50 g) cornflour (cornstarch) and 1½ tablespoons baking powder

Combine the ingredients and sift together three times. Basically, sift the flours back and forth between two mixing bowls. Sifting not only mixes the ingredients together appropriately, it aerates the mixture so the consistency is similar to that of real cake flour.

TIPS

If the recipe requires more cake flour, you can do this process in bulk, but I find it's better to make each batch of cake flour separately.

Cornflour is extra fine and lowers the gluten formation in the plain flour, similar to cake flour. In some countries, cornflour is referred to as cornstarch. Make sure you are not using cornmeal – they are completely different ingredients.

STORAGE

Store in an airtight container in a cool, dry place until ready to use.

SALTED CARAMEL

MAKES 3 CUPS (750 ML) **GF**

Salted caramel is dangerously addictive and no doubt you'll find many reasons to use it in your sweet creations! You can make salted caramel tarts, truffles, cakes and puddings or use it as a topping on ice cream or cheesecake. It's perfect for storing in the refrigerator for when dessert calls. It is also a luxurious condiment for making ahead and gifting to loved ones.

2 cups (440 g) caster (superfine) sugar

185 g (6½ oz) unsalted butter, chopped

1 cup (250 ml) thick (double) cream

2 teaspoons sea salt

STORAGE

Salted caramel can be stored in an airtight container and refrigerated for up to 2 weeks or frozen for up to 2 months.

1 Heat the sugar in a medium saucepan over medium heat, stirring constantly with a silicone spatula or wooden spoon. The sugar will form clumps and eventually melt into a thick, amber–brown coloured liquid as you continue to stir.

2 Once the sugar is completely melted, immediately add the butter. Be careful in this step because the caramel will bubble rapidly when the butter is added. Stir the butter into the caramel until it is completely melted, about 2–3 minutes.

3 Continue stirring as you very slowly drizzle in the cream. (Because the cream is colder than the caramel, the mixture will rapidly bubble and splatter when added.) Allow the mixture to boil for 1 minute – it will rise in the pan as it boils.

4 Remove the saucepan from the heat and stir in the salt, to taste. Allow the salted caramel to cool completely before using. (For a thinner consistency, stir in more cream.)

TIP See p. 84 for a vegan caramel recipe.

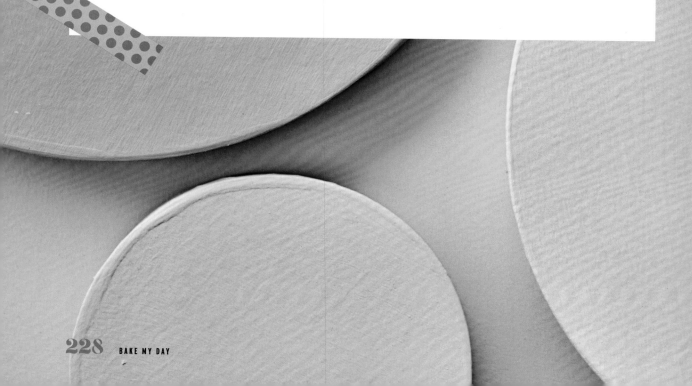

DULCE DE LECHE

MAKES 2 CUPS (500 ML)

Thick and glossy, richly creamy and sweet, this spreadable golden caramel turns simple treats into luxurious desserts. It's utterly luscious and I always make sure I have a jar of dulce de leche on hand (either homemade or store-bought). Here is a relatively fast way to make dulce de leche at home. Instead of boiling cans of condensed milk for 3 hours (plus 4 hours cooling time) like many recipes suggest, you can simply bake the sweetened condensed milk in the oven until it turns into a thick golden caramel — and the whisking speeds up the cooling time.

Spoon dulce de leche into mini pastry cases or use it as a filling for banoffee pie, swirl it through your favourite cheesecake, serve it with pancakes or French toast, heat it up and drizzle it over ice cream, use it as a filling for cakes (my favourite) or as a spread for biscuits. You can also serve it with other South American and Spanish specialties, like churros!

800 g (1 lb 12 oz) tinned sweetened condensed milk (I use Nestlé brand)

1 teaspoon vanilla bean paste (optional, but it gives the dulce de leche a richer flavour)

1   Preheat the oven to 220°C (425°F) fan-forced. Pour the sweetened condensed milk and vanilla into an ovenproof baking dish. Place the dish in a roasting pan and pour water into the pan to come halfway up the side of the baking dish.

2   Cover the baking dish with foil and bake, refilling the pan with water if necessary, for 1 hour 45 minutes, or until the dulce de leche is dark golden in colour.

3   Using a hand-held mixer or stick blender, whisk the warm caramel in the baking dish until it is smooth.

4   Pour the dulce de leche into a 2-cup (500 ml) capacity sterilised jar and allow it to cool before sealing.

STORAGE

This dulce de leche can be stored in the refrigerator unopened for 2 months. Once opened, it can be stored in the refrigerator for up to 3 weeks.

GOLDEN PEANUT BRITTLE

SERVES 30

A touch of salt and some dusted edible gold give this trusty peanut brittle recipe a luxurious glow-up! I use this golden peanut brittle as a fancy decoration for cakes, loaves, cupcakes, ice cream sundaes, tarts, everything! Or package it up into little gift bags (mixed with buttery popcorn and chocolate-covered pretzels) and send them out to your family and friends.

1 cup (140 g) salted roast peanuts

2½ cups (550 g) caster (superfine) sugar

50 g (1¾ oz) unsalted butter, at room temperature

1 teaspoon edible gold powder, to decorate (available from cake decorating stores; optional)

STORAGE

This peanut brittle can be stored in an airtight container lined with baking paper, with baking paper between each layer of brittle, in a cool, dry place for up to 7 days.

1   Line an 18 x 28 cm (7 x 11¼ inch) slice tin, at least 3 cm (1¼ inches) deep, with baking paper. Spread the nuts over the base.

2   Combine the sugar and ½ cup (125 ml) water in a saucepan. Stir over medium heat until the sugar dissolves, then bring to the boil. Gently boil, occasionally brushing down the side of the saucepan with a pastry brush dipped in water to dissolve any sugar crystals, for 25 minutes, or until it is a rich golden colour.

3   Remove the saucepan from the heat and stir in the butter with a wooden spoon or silicone spatula until just combined.

4   Quickly pour the toffee mixture into the prepared tin (it won't fill it completely). Set aside in a cool place until the toffee sets, around 20 minutes.

5   Dust with the edible gold powder (if using) and break the brittle into pieces.

TIP   A candy thermometer will reach 170°C (325°F) when the sugar syrup is ready.

PRESSED EDIBLE FLOWERS

MAKES 30-40

You may have made pressed flowers in the past for creating all kinds of beautiful items, from adorning homemade cards to decorating your home, but have you ever thought to add your pressed creations to a cake? Pressed edible flowers can help you create a truly impressive work of natural art! Place the pressed flowers directly onto a cake frosted with buttercream or use them to make stunning crystal flower lollipops. When adorning a cake with edible flowers, using a variety of pressed flowers will create an aesthetically beautiful cake that looks more organic.

large old book (that you don't
   mind ruining if the pages
   warp because of moisture)

sheets of white paper cut
   to size (to absorb moisture
   from the flowers)

punnet of edible flowers
   (available from specialty
   grocers and online)

brick or very heavy object

1 Open the book and line opposite pages with white paper that has been cut to size. I usually start from the middle of the book and spread the pages of pressed flowers throughout. Place flowers onto one of the pages and turn the page. Next, carefully open another page (being mindful not to disturb the other pages filled with flowers) and repeat this process until you've pressed as many flowers (plus extra!) as you think you may need for the cake decorating.

2 Leave the book closed in a cool dry setting (away from any disturbances) and press flat with a brick. To achieve a flat and pressed effect, leave the flowers to set for at least 3 days.

TIP You can also buy dried and pre-pressed edible flowers, as well as freeze-dried flowers. You can find these online, in some specialty grocers and from cake decorating stores.

STORAGE

The pressed edible flowers can be made at least 1 month in advance. Store in an airtight container, in a cool and dry place, away from direct sunlight.

MERINGUE KISSES

MAKES 40 MINI KISSES OR 10 LARGER SMOOCHES

This is my foolproof recipe created especially to make easy meringue kisses. I use meringue kisses to artfully adorn tarts, cakes, cupcakes and any other desserts needing some luxurious flair! You can tint them a variety of colours and add any water-based flavouring extracts you like. These meringue kisses are wonderfully crunchy and melt away blissfully in your mouth.

6 (180 g) large egg whites
   (pasteurised egg
   whites are available in
   cartons at most major
   supermarkets), chilled

½ teaspoon cream of tartar

1⅔ cup (360 g) caster
   (superfine) sugar

½ teaspoon vanilla
   bean paste

medium–large piping
   bag fitted with a 1 cm
   (½ inch) round nozzle

STORAGE

You can make the meringues 1 week ahead of time and store them in an airtight container in a dry environment until needed for assembly.

1 Preheat the oven to 100°C (200°F) fan-forced and line a baking tray with baking paper.

2 Using a hand-held mixer or a stand mixer fitted with the whisk attachment, whisk the egg whites and cream of tartar on medium speed for around 2 minutes, or until foamy and just beginning to turn white.

3 While continuing to whisk, add the sugar very slowly (about 1 teaspoon at a time).

4 When all the sugar has been added, turn the mixer up to high speed and whisk for around 5 minutes, or until the meringue is glossy and very stiff. Mix in the vanilla on high for around 10 seconds.

5 Fill the piping bag with the meringue mixture, then hold the piping bag vertically over the baking tray, almost touching the tray. Squeeze out a small amount of meringue to form the base, then gently and swiftly lift the piping bag upwards so that a nice tip is formed. Pipe the kisses onto the baking tray leaving a 1 cm (½ inch) gap between each.

6 Bake the meringues in the oven for 2–2½ hours, or until light and crisp (do not brown). Turn the oven off and leave the meringues in the oven with the door ajar to cool to room temperature.

TIP When making meringues, make sure that both the mixing bowl and whisk are clean and dry, as any moisture or fat will stop the egg whites from forming a meringue. It is also important to add the sugar slowly or the meringue will collapse.

PERFECT SWISS MERINGUE BUTTERCREAM

MAKES 10 CUPS (2.5 LITRES)

Through years of making and eating countless variations of frostings, cream cheeses and buttercreams, I've found meringue-based buttercreams create the smoothest finish. I enjoy making Swiss meringue buttercream in my kitchen – it is silky smooth and fluffy, extremely stable for stacking multiple cake layers, and tastes simply divine.

2½ cups (550 g) caster (superfine) sugar

10 large egg whites (pasteurised egg whites are available in cartons at most major supermarkets), chilled

900 g (2 lb) unsalted butter, softened to a spreadable consistency

2 teaspoons vanilla bean paste

STORAGE

Cover the bowl with plastic wrap and set aside in a cool, dry place until needed. You can refrigerate this buttercream for up to 10 days or freeze for up to 2 months. Thaw frozen buttercream overnight in the refrigerator, then bring to room temperature (gently reheat in the microwave in 20-second bursts if needed). Beat the buttercream on low speed until smooth before applying to your cake.

1 Place the sugar and egg whites in a heatproof glass bowl. Set the bowl over a saucepan of gently simmering water, and whisk until the sugar has dissolved and the egg whites are slightly warm to the touch (at least 40°C/104°F). (You can omit this step entirely if you are using pasteurised egg whites, and instead, simply place the sugar and egg whites directly into the mixer.)

2 Transfer the mixture into the bowl of a stand mixer fitted with the whisk attachment. Whisk on high speed until the mixture has formed stiff and glossy peaks, around 10–15 minutes.

3 Switch to the paddle attachment. Add the butter in thirds, and beat on high speed after each addition until incorporated. Don't be alarmed if the buttercream appears curdled – it will become light and fluffy again with continued beating for around 2–3 minutes (I absolutely promise!). Add the vanilla bean paste and beat until just combined.

4 The buttercream is now ready to be used. Follow individual recipes for instructions on how to tint and flavour further. If you are making buttercream ahead of time and you find there are bubbles visible when you come to use it, you may need to mix it further before use. Using a stand mixer fitted with the paddle attachment, beat on low speed for 2–3 minutes to eliminate the air bubbles.

TIP See p. 170 for a vegan vanilla buttercream recipe.

acknowledgements

The whole process of creating a cake or dessert for the people you love is such a wonderful and generous way to celebrate a special occasion. So I'm just thrilled at the thought of you fellow treat-loving friends taking these recipes and making them memorable in your very own way! I am hugely grateful to my beautiful readers (here's raising a lemon meringue tartlet kiss to YOU) for supporting me in the creation of my third cookbook. You continue to keep this ridiculously fun dream of living my best 'cake life' alive. I owe you all the heartfelt hugs and high-fives in the world!

Behind every great cookbook is a diverse and passionate team of highly talented people. My cookbook family at Murdoch Books (and more specifically Allen & Unwin) have once again expertly held my mixing bowl throughout this entire fun-filled process, facilitating my wildest home-baking dreams. To Jane, Megan, Virginia, Emma, Jeremy, Kerrie, Martine, Sarah (as well as countless others behind the scenes): honestly, I couldn't have asked to work with a more thorough, imaginative or hilarious group of people and it's just been the best! The pages within this book speak louder to this sentiment than I ever could right here.

When it comes to creativity in food, my Vietnamese-born Mum and my late German grandmother, Liselotte, are brilliant cooks and have always created meals and desserts with whichever ingredients they've had on hand. Recipes (while they're excellent guidelines) aren't gospel in our family, and the challenge of resourcefulness is not only exciting but rewardingly delicious! Worst case scenario, if the culinary experiment 'bombs', we always have my dad, Hans, hungrily waiting to eat the evidence! I think this approach to food has greatly influenced my philosophy that there shouldn't be hard rules when it comes to cooking for the people you love, so long as you know you're using good quality ingredients and, of course,

it tastes good too. We've triple-taste-tested all of the recipes in this cookbook for you just to be sure.

To my loving family and my trusted circle of beautifully diverse friends, I'm so lucky to be a part of such a vibrant community of people. Thanks for cheering on my quirks and idiosyncrasies. It's always our uniqueness and difference that makes us all so interesting! I like to think of cakes as having their own little personalities too, because life is much more fun that way.

A heartfelt thank you to my hunky other half, Troy, for your unwavering thoughtfulness and for consistently feeding me the best home-cooked savoury food when the cake lady can no longer bear to be in the kitchen (I love food but my stove-top patience seems to begin and end with sweets). At the time of writing this acknowledgements section, Troy and I are overjoyed to be 5 months pregnant with our first child. It's been really special shooting the pages of this cookbook with our new little sous chef baking away at the same time, and the support throughout this process from darling Troy as well as the cookbook dream team has been truly energising.

*Bake My Day i*s for anyone whose encouragement, friendship, and kindness has allowed me to kick some major home baking goals within the golden shores of this beautiful country and beyond. The feeling of seeing home-baked treats being shared around the globe with the sole purpose of making people happy is just PURE BLISS. Don't ever forget, a friendly local home baker (aka cake dealer) such as yourself always has the ability to bake the world a better place. Cheers for inviting this cookbook to your next party and for baking my day!

Kat xo

INDEX

Published in 2022 by Murdoch Books, an imprint of Allen & Unwin

Murdoch Books Australia
83 Alexander Street
Crows Nest NSW 2065
Phone: +61 (0)2 8425 0100
murdochbooks.com.au
info@murdochbooks.com.au

Murdoch Books UK
Ormond House
26–27 Boswell Street
London WC1N 3JZ
Phone: +44 (0) 20 8785 5995
murdochbooks.co.uk
info@murdochbooks.co.uk

For corporate orders and custom publishing, contact our business development team
at salesenquiries@murdochbooks.com.au

Publisher: Jane Morrow
Editorial Manager: Virginia Birch
Design Manager: Megan Pigott
Designer/illustrator: Julia Cornelius
Editor: Martine Lleonart
Photographer: Jeremy Simons
Stylist: Emma Knowles
Home Economist: Kerrie Ray
Production Director: Lou Playfair

Text © Katherine Sabbath 2022
The moral right of the author has
been asserted.
Design © Murdoch Books 2022
Photography © Jeremy Simons 2022

*We acknowledge that we meet and work on the traditional lands of the Cammeraygal
people of the Eora Nation and pay our respects to their elders past, present and future.*

ISBN 978 1 92261 601 2 Australia
ISBN 978 1 91166 854 1 UK

A catalogue record for this
book is available from the
National Library of Australia

A catalogue record for this book is available from the British Library

Colour reproduction by Splitting Image Colour Studio Pty Ltd, Clayton, Victoria
Printed by C&C Offset Printing Co. Ltd., China

OVEN GUIDE: These recipes have all been tested in a fan-forced oven. You may find cooking times vary
depending on the oven you are using.

TABLESPOON MEASURES: We have used 20 ml (4 teaspoon) tablespoon measures. If you are using
a 15 ml (3 teaspoon) tablespoon add an extra teaspoon of the ingredient for each tablespoon specified.

IMPORTANT: Those who might be at risk from the effects of salmonella poisoning (the elderly, pregnant women,
young children and those suffering from immune deficiency diseases) should consult their doctor with any
concerns about eating raw eggs.

10 9 8 7 6 5 4 3 2 1